RIT - WALLACE LIBRARY
CIRCULATING LIBRARY BOOKS

OVERDUE FINES AND FEES FOR <u>ALL</u> BORROWERS

*Recalled = $1/ day overdue (no grace period)
*Billed = $10.00/ item when returned 4 or more weeks overdue
*Lost Items = replacement cost+$10 fee
*All materials must be returned or renewed by the duedate.

Management and Entrepreneurism

■ SMART STRATEGIES SERIES ■

Management and Entrepreneurism

John C. Chicken

THOMSON

————★——— ™

LEARNING   Australia • Canada • Mexico • Singapore • Spain • United Kingdom • United States

THOMSON

LEARNING

Management and Entrepreneurism

Copyright © 2000 John C. Chicken

Thomson Learning™ is a trademark used herein under licence.

For more information, contact Thomson Learning, Berkshire House, 168–173 High Holborn, London, WC1V 7AA or visit us on the World Wide Web at: http://www.thomsonlearning.co.uk

British Library Cataloguing-in-Publication Data
A catalogue record for this book is available from the British Library

ISBN 1-86152-639-3

First edition published 2000 by Thomson Learning

Typeset by LaserScript Limited, Mitcham, Surrey
Printed in the UK by TJ International, Padstow, Cornwall
Cover design by Words and Pictures

Contents

List of figures

List of tables

Preface

The aim of this book is to provide all concerned with establishing or updating management systems with the essential tools for constructive critical assessment of the adequacy of systems proposed. Special attention is given to identifying the extent to which entrepreneurism can be exploited for the good of a country as a whole. Both public and private sectors are considered, particular attention being given to identifying:

- features common to both sectors;

- differences between the two sectors; and

- the impact of interfaces between the two sectors.

It is hoped that the book will be useful to those studying management and give some useful insights to those studying politics and those concerned with decision making at the political level.

Throughout the book care is taken to expose where and how action is constrained. The forms of constraints considered include legislation, markets, conventions, resistance to change and size of organisation. Care has also been taken to illustrate the arguments with cases based closely on real world events.

In all the arguments presented, an attempt has been made to expose whether or not there is real benefit to the country as a whole in greater adoption of entrepreneurism. Possible benefits are considered to be reduction in taxes, goods produced being cheaper, services cheaper and projects being brought to fruition faster.

The argument is built up in eight main steps which are:

1   The nature of activities requiring management

2   The forms of entrepreneurism

3   The forms of management

4   The real and imaginary constraints on management action

5   The reality of management in local government

6   The reality of management in central government

7   The reality of management and entrepreneurism in the private sector

8   Where improvements in management efficiency can be made

It is hoped by arranging the study in this way the reader will appreciate the implications for decision making of the real world constraints. Allowing for constraints as early as possible in any kind of project can ultimately help to bring it to completion in the shortest time.

There are several important topics mentioned in the main text that need a little more discussion than would be appropriate there, so they have been included as appendices. These appendices are likely to be particularly helpful to students of management. The appendices are:

1   The problems of selecting managers

2   The nature of quality assurance controls

3   Assessment of the acceptability of projects

4   Social cost-benefit analysis

CHAPTER ONE

Introduction

In the real world there is often misplaced optimism about the benefits to be achieved from improved management and the application of entrepreneurism. The optimism is misplaced because the difficulties of overcoming the constraints associated with the activity of interest are underestimated. It is often hoped that a little tinkering with the system or using a few 'buzz-words' or 'in-phrases' will instantly bring about the improvements in efficiency required. For any activity to be developed in the most efficient way possible it is essential that the constraints involved are fully understood. Any plans to improve efficiency must identify the action that should be taken to deal with constraints so that the benefits of entrepreneurism can be fully exploited.

This book attempts to identify the nature of constraints and the role for management in trying to extract the maximum benefit from entrepreneurism. It is not intended to follow the F.W. Taylor approach of suggesting improvement in efficiency can be achieved simply by eliminating waste and ensuring everyone works to the maximum of their capability, but to look at the whole range of constraints managers have to overcome to reap the maximum benefit from each activity (Burnham and Bramley 1950: 8). Also it is not intended to slavishly follow the teaching of any other management gurus. However, attention is drawn to the implications of the changing nature of society. The importance is stressed of looking to the future and how future demands are to be satisfied.

The problem of minimising the impact of constraints is a complex one that managers, politicians and policy makers must understand and devote considerable effort to solving, as soon as possible in the life of a proposal. The solutions adopted must be those that allow the activities involved to be developed in the most efficient way possible. By its very nature minimising constraints involves managers, lawyers, politicians, economists, civil servants, engineers, financiers, local, national and international legislation, and the whole range of pressure groups. Without being too cynical the problem could be described as overcoming entrenched conventions to produce a better life. A rather picturesque way of describing the approach required is to say it is a problem like convincing the cavalry generals that to defeat tanks the conventional cavalry weapons of sabre and lance must be changed.

The approach I have adopted in this book is to show the nature of the problem and the action required to arrive at the most effective solution. This, it is hoped, will show the reader the essential features of good management and entrepreneurism. The approach adopted is pragmatic and all I ask of readers is that they approach the subject with an open critical enquiring mind that is not hidebound by conventions. The approach is mainly non-mathematical but does require some understanding of elementary statistics. The examination is divided into eight parts, each part being presented in a separate chapter. The presentation is designed to provide the management student and the operational manager with a set of tools that will help them identify the problems and the most efficient way of dealing with them.

In Chapter 2 the nature of the roles managers are likely to have to play are described in general terms and attention is drawn to the spectra of skills likely to be required to satisfy the various functions they have to perform. Managers in both large and small private and public organisations are considered, with attention being given to the significance of the differences and similarities of the different types of organisation. From this identification of the spectra of skills and roles involved an attempt is made to extract the features common to all management operations. Particular attention is drawn to the composition of the environment surrounding management activities. Important among the components considered are technical, economic and socio-political factors.

In Chapter 3 entrepreneurism is analysed and attention is focused on the many differences between entrepreneurism in the public sector and entrepreneurism in the private sector. This leads to consideration of the interaction of entrepreneurism between the two sectors.

As with the consideration of the operational environment in Chapter 2, attention is given in this chapter to the operational environment in which entrepreneurial activity has to operate. Particular attention is drawn to the differences in the composition of the environment associated with operations in the public and private sectors.

In Chapter 4 an attempt is made to give a summary of the whole matrix of management techniques available and to identify where they fit into the framework of developing maximum efficiency and effectiveness of an organisation. This chapter begins to expose the constraints on action that management can take. Special attention is given to the importance of managers assessing the future needs of their organisation and taking positive steps to ensure that their organisations are, as far as practical, prepared for the future.

Chapter 5 begins with a simple examination of constraints identified in Chapter 4 and then analyses their impact. Attention is given to both the real constraints, that is those that have some basis in the real world, and those that are imaginary. Imaginary constraints are those that are based on convention and those that have developed by custom. Such imaginary constraints can be very real and difficult barriers to overcome.

Chapter 6 examines the reality of management in local government. The examination exposes the way such organisations are constrained by legislation and the pressures of elected members. Important conclusions of this chapter are that the efficiency of local government could be improved by rationalisation of the organisation of local government and giving managers freedom in the way they finance their activities.

Chapter 7 looks at the reality of management in central government and examines the way the processes of central government impact on management and entrepreneurism of activities in the private sector.

Chapter 8 looks at the reality of management and entrepreneurism in the private sector. The argument is illustrated by three case studies. These case studies expose the nature and impact of the interactions between government bodies and the private sector.

Chapter 9 attempts to draw from earlier chapters ways in which management can be improved and entrepreneurism can be exploited to a more beneficial extent.

Chapter 10 attempts to (1) critically summarise the arguments in the earlier chapters, (2) draw attention to the controversial aspects of the arguments presented, (3) assess the possible advantages of the approach described.

To amplify the arguments in some chapters and to provide additional background material, four appendices to the main text are included:

Appendix 1   The problems of selecting managers.
              This appendix explains the problem of selecting managers and describes one way of collecting and comparing the information about the various applicants considered.
Appendix 2   The nature of quality assurance controls.
              This appendix examines the requirements of quality

assurance management controls, obstacles to effective use of quality assurance management and the results of introducing effective quality assurance management.

Appendix 3   Describes one methodology that can be used to determine the acceptability of the costs involved in making a project acceptable.

Appendix 4   Examines the problems of making an analysis of socio cost-benefit implications of proposals.

An important overall conclusion of the study is that it draws attention to the advantages of a well-informed, critical, open-minded analytical approach to solving the problems of improving the efficiency of government, industry and society as a whole.

References

Burnham, T.H. and Bramley, D.H. (1950) *Engineering Economics Book II*, 6th edn, London: Sir Isaac Pitman and Sons Ltd, p. 8.

CHAPTER TWO

The nature of activities requiring management

The discussion of management that follows is designed not to be restricted to management of any particular activity. My aim has been to make the results of the examination of management systems applicable, with adjustment, to all activities. My justification for this approach is that in my experience although there are minor differences in management styles for particular activities there is an essential common core in all management processes regardless of the activity involved.

The basic nature of all management functions is, regardless of the activity, to ensure in an enduring way that a particular input is converted into the required output. Thus the details of the management process are defined by the output required, which may be similar in many activities and not unique to any particular activity. A sample of activities that require some form of management is summarised in Table 2.1, together with the forms of management required. From Table 2.1 it can be clearly seen how the management functions required for many activities have many common features. It is appreciated that the list of activities is not comprehensive: for example, medical services, elected politicians and voluntary services are not included. Also it is appreciated that although the nature of the management functions employed may be similar, the technical content of the function has to be carefully adapted to each activity. A dramatic example of this adjustment process is the difference in the criteria to be set for recruiting pilots for the airforce and the criteria set for recruiting shepherds for a hill farm. In both cases a suitable person has to be selected, but for each job very different characteristics are required. Similarly accounting in a government department is rather different to accounting in a commercial organisation. In Table 2.2 an attempt is made to summarise the range of characteristics of the main management functions.

One function that illustrates, in a very direct way, all the activities of management is ensuring that contracts are satisfied. It is therefore helpful

TABLE 2.1 Summary of the range of management functions required for a sample of activities

Activity	Range of management functions required
Armed forces	Purchasing, recruitment, accounting, training, planning, negotiating with government bodies
Financial institutions	Purchasing, sales, training, recruitment, accounting, planning, negotiating with government bodies
Manufacturing industries	Purchasing, sales, training, accounting, planning, recruitment and negotiating with government bodies
Transport	Purchasing, sales, training, accounting, planning, recruitment and negotiating with government bodies
Agriculture	Purchasing, sales, training, accounting, planning, recruitment and negotiating with government bodies
Mining	Purchasing, sales, training, accounting, planning, recruitment and negotiating with government bodies
Fishing	Purchasing, sales, training, accounting, planning, recruitment and negotiating with government bodies
Hotels	Purchasing, sales, training, accounting, planning, recruitment and negotiating with government bodies
Media	Purchasing, sales, training, accounting, planning, recruitment and negotiating with government bodies
Civil service	Purchasing, training, accounting, planning, recruitment, negotiating with government bodies and dealing with elected members
Local government	Purchasing, training, accounting, planning, recruitment, negotiating with government bodies and dealing with elected members

to use that activity as an illustration of the essential nature of the management function. In the following the main steps in satisfying a contract are examined in some detail. In Figure 2.1 the main steps in satisfying a contract are set out in the form of a flow sheet. The diagram is a gross simplification of reality, but it does show how in most activities the essential role of management is solving problems in a way that allows the basic aims of the activity to be satisfied.

Defects or weaknesses in the management and organisation of completion of a contract are often manifest in cost overruns and delays. Defence contracts give some dramatic examples of the magnitude of cost overruns and delays. For the period up to March 1998 it was reported that 25 top Ministry of Defence projects are expected to cost £2.8 billion more than originally forecast ('MoD to act on costs and delays' 1999: 7). It was

TABLE 2.2   Summary of the main management function characteristics

Function	Characteristics
Ensuring that contracts are satisfied	Understanding what action has to be taken and the priorities that have to be satisfied
Dealing with emergencies	A plan of action for dealing with various types of emergencies and ensuring that business interruptions are kept to a minimum
Purchasing	A knowledge of what is required, the use it will be put to, potential suppliers and prices
Recruitment	A clear understanding of the capability, competence and experience and the relevant legislation
Accounting	Understanding of income and expenditure, sources of income and accounting procedures
Training	Knowledge of skills employees require and where they can be obtained. Systematic approach to development of appropriate skills
Planning	Development of a structured approach to the tasks that have to be completed so that they can be dealt with in the most efficient way possible. Also determining what future requirements may have to be dealt with and how they may be dealt with
Negotiating with government bodies	Knowledge and understanding of the government bodies, function, constraints on their operations and their method of working
Sales	Knowledge of what has to be sold, the market, customers and the local business procedure
Dealing with elected members	Although this is very important for national and local government officials, it is also important for all organisations dealing with government officials and elected members to have a knowledge of elected members' interests, roles and influence

also reported that on average the projects will enter service 3½ years later than originally planned. Eight of the 25 projects were more than five years late and one project was likely to be ten years late. Such delays and cost overruns are not peculiar to the defence industry, they happen with many types of contract. Another example from a quite unrelated field is the National Health Service Executive's Phase 3 development at Guy's Hospital, which saw the costs rise from the original estimate of £35.5 million to £150.6 million ('NHS managers warned on PFI cost overruns' 1999: 8). In fact it would be more precise to say the problems may arise with every type of contract. So the central questions are: what are the

FIGURE 2.1 The main steps in satisfying a contract

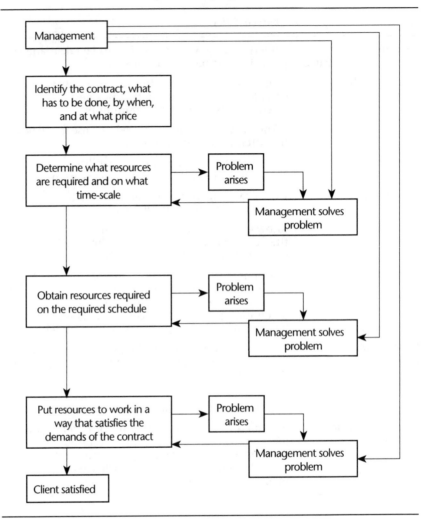

causes of such delays and cost overruns and how can such problems be avoided in the future?

The client has a basic responsibility for dealing with such issues and should ask five basic questions about the competence and capability of the staff placing such contracts. The questions are:

1   Do the staff responsible for placing such contracts understand the nature and magnitude of the technical issues that have to be dealt with?

2   Do the staff responsible for managing the contract know how all the technical problems involved can be solved?

3   If the staff do not understand the problems and how the problems can be solved, are there experts available who can answer these questions?

4   Does the contractor selected really have the competences to solve the problems, or did he/she just submit a low price with the intention of building up a suitably competent team once the contract was awarded?

5   Is the task specified in the contract so novel that no realistic estimate of time to completion or cost can be made?

It is not unknown in the tender process for a potential contractor to make a bid so low that it will ensure they get the contract. They make such a low bid on the basis that they know they will be able to cover the real cost by making claims for additional payments during the life of the contract. There are of course contractual measures that can be tried to avoid overspend or delays in completion. These measures include:

1   Fixed price contracts.

2   Bonus for early completion.

3   Fines for late completion.

Suitable contractors may be well aware of the market value of their unique specialist knowledge and be unwilling to accept a contract that could put them at a financial disadvantage.

The type of contract used has to be adapted to the work to be done, also both parties have to understand the obligation that the contract places on them.

Contracts are just one type of problem management has to solve.

The word problem is used in a generous way to include a very wide range of issues, but what does it mean in practice? The spectrum of problems that managers have to deal with is very broad. The spectrum varies not only within a particular activity but also for each type of activity. The problems range from staff having to be able to deal with the consequences of vital staff suddenly dying to having to deal with climatic disasters like floods and hurricanes. Table 2.3 gives a summary of the range of problems management must be prepared to deal with. Ideally management should have some plans ready for dealing with all problem situations that may arise. Such plans may only exist in outline, but at

TABLE 2.3   Summary of the types of problems management may have to deal with

Generic problem	Examples	Management action
Risk assessment and management	High risk of finance not being available	Identify alternative sources of finance
Human resources	Vital staff ill Staff on strike Staff do not have appropriate skills	Develop access to temporary staff and capability to relocate project
Equipment	Equipment breaks down Computers fail Equipment not suitable for job	Have alternative sources of equipment available
Material supply	Supply problems Material defective Specification changes	Alternative suppliers identified Alternative materials proved to satisfy specification
Wars/riots	Changes in demand Buildings damaged Staff killed, working time lost	Plans for relocations Arrangement for alternative staff Plans for recovery
Government policy	New requirements have to be satisfied Additional paperwork introduced Products have to change	Monitor government proposals carefully to assess implications for activities and have a plan for dealing with the new situation
Finance	Cost of borrowing changes Extra taxes on supplies Loans recalled	Have alternative sources of cheaper finance ready Find ways of reducing finance required
Client/customer relations	Customer goes bankrupt Customers change requirements Customers pay slowly	Look for alternative markets Assess customers carefully
Climate	Floods Earthquakes Hurricanes Storms	Emergency plans ready for dealing with problem and business recovery

least management should not have to start building plans from scratch every time a problem arises. In large firms the plans for dealing with problems may be set out in the company management manual.

The central feature for all management plans for dealing with emergency problems is that they aim to keep the activity involved going.

TABLE 2.4 Summary of the components of management's plans for dealing with problems

Component's place in problem solving plan	Nature of component	Essential features of component
1	Overall plan	Identifies action, people, equipment and funding required
2	Establishing lines of communication that sense and report the emergence of problems	It is vital that problems are detected as soon as possible. It is often easier to deal with problems as they are emerging rather than when they have emerged
3	Identifying problem solving/ emergency response team. These are the people who must take action to deal in a co-ordinated way with various aspects of solving the problem	Co-ordination of the response is essential as it prevents duplication of effort and essential actions being overlooked
4	Co-ordinated action taken by the problem solving/ emergency response team.	The action taken must be such that the organisation is able to satisfy its aims with the minimum of disturbance or delay
5	Critically review the efficiency of the response to problem solving situations	The critical review should identify where improvements can be made

In the private sector this may mean identifying action required to stay in business. In a government organisation this may mean identifying the action required to keep the organisation functioning or at least arranging for the organisation's function to be satisfied in some way. That is a very broad statement of what management's approach to dealing with emergency problems must be. In reality there are many components of this approach and their role and importance must be understood. In Table 2.4 the main components of any plan for dealing with emergency problems are summarised in a way that sets out the order in which they are likely to be required. No attempt is made to specify the precise action required.

To illustrate the nature of the problems that may have to be dealt with, two very simplified real-world cases are now described:

TABLE 2.5 Major problems related to two case studies

Multi-purpose fighter/bomber case

Problem	Action	Response to problems involved
Planning	Identifying when action is required and when it can be taken	When will government funding be available. How will pre-contract work be funded
Resources	Design team must be adequate Experimental facilities to provide proof of design must be adequate Obtain adequate finance	Looking for other more secure ways of financing the project. Perhaps consider getting a consortium of counties to finance the project. Design staff must be recruited and trained
Start of project	The start of government funding agreed. Unless the company involved has very large financial resources starting the design without a clear financial commitment from the government is likely to generate financial problems for the company	Delays may result in project being out of date before it is started. Design specification may be changed by client. A change in government policy may stop the project. Very careful assessment of proposed project before making a major commitment to starting the project

Oil Refinery proposal case

Problem	Action	Response to problems involved
Planning	Deciding when refining capacity is required by and when planning approval is required by	Pattern of demand for product determined which in turn sets target for when plant must be complete and operational
Resources	Design team to prepare layout and specification. Lawyers to deal with legal side of getting planning approval. Economists to evaluate financial implications	Oil company able to finance construction of refinery construction from its own resources
Start of project	Site approval required before construction can start. If a public inquiry is involved exactly when construction may start will be uncertain	If getting planning approval is delayed the delay may be unacceptable to the oil company and they may decide to locate plant elsewhere

TABLE 2.6 Possible approaches to dealing with the problems in two cases

Multi-purpose fighter/bomber case

Time-scale	Approach
Short term	Prepare a very elementary design to base tender on. This would be a low initial cost approach but it is likely to give an unreliable indication of the cost. Alternatively look for partners to share cost or provide additional finance
Long term	Improve firm's finance for research, development and preliminary design. Find alternative sources of income which might result in drastic change to product line

Oil Refinery proposal case

Time-scale	Approach
Short term	Determine how long it will take to get planning approval. If delays are unacceptable find an alternative site for refinery. This may involve siting the refinery in a different country
Long term	Assess whether there are more cost-effective sites for refineries and are there locations where planning permission can be obtained quickly and easily, without recourse to drawn-out public inquiries. Investigate the possibility of reducing the size of refinery plant for the same throughput

1   An aircraft company hoping to win a contract to design and build a new multi-purpose fighter/bomber.

2   An oil company wanting to build an oil refinery on a site close to a large residential development.

The problems associated with these two cases are summarised in Table 2.5. Possible approaches to dealing with the problems are set out in Table 2.6. The tables show how solving the immediate problems will often expose in a very direct way long-term issues which should be addressed and if solved could be of lasting benefit to the organisation involved.

The cases also show that problem solving is a continuous dynamic process for management in any organisation. To suggest that problem solving is an adequate description of all management activities is grossly misleading. The real art of good management is to anticipate problems and to ensure action is taken to minimise their adverse impact on an organisation's activities. Table 2.7 identifies some of the possible problem issues management might reasonably be expected to anticipate and have plans for dealing with before they arise. The list is only a sample of the possible range of problems. With each of the management functions, such as those already identified in Table 2.2, there may be several problem areas that have to be dealt with.

This brings out the question of exactly how should the manager's role be played. As defined at the beginning of this chapter, a manager has to be the person responsible for ensuring that a task/activity is undertaken in a way that satisfies the goals set for it. The role a manager plays is constrained by many factors, a sample of which are listed in Table 2.8. Some of the factors are direct and some indirect. It is not in any way suggested that the direct factors are more important than the indirect. Some of the more important direct factors are identified in Table 2.9. Indirect factors are hard to define with precision, but their cumulative effect can be dramatic. Table 2.10 identifies some of the more important indirect factors.

TABLE 2.7 Problems that management might be expected to anticipate and deal with before they become a crisis

Problem area	Possible anticipatory action
Shortage of materials	Study the market and assess the significance and impact of changes in the supply system
Shortage of skilled staff	Increasing demand for product might indicate increase in production which in turn might show a shortage of staff with suitable skills. One solution might be to increase in-house training to produce the required staff
Customers paying late giving rise to cash flow problems	Insert a clause in all contracts setting out the need for all invoices to be paid promptly and the meaning of promptly clearly defined
Delays in government contracts being signed	Make sure that finances are adequate to cover delays and that potential clients understand all the implications of delays
Sales staff are not developing the market as fully as expected	Monitor sales performance very carefully. Have plans for improving sales performance

TABLE 2.8   Some of the factors that constrain the role a manager plays

Factor	Influence
Size of organisation	Large organisation likely to have many managers with various specialist skills. A small company may have just one manager (who may be the owner) and responsible for everything
Position of manager	Manager may be just in charge of a very small department. The manager of interest in this study will have overall responsibility for an activity
Duty of manager (running a department of a whole company)	The type of manager considered in this study will be able to influence the firm's policy, quality and quantity of output.
Type of product of the organisation involved	The influence of the type of product is profound, for example a manager in an accountant's office requires different skills to someone running a car factory
Skill of the person called a manager	A manager in any field must have a complete understanding of that field, otherwise he/she will not be able to anticipate problems and identify ways of dealing with them
Skill level of the people to be managed	The skill level of the people who have to be managed has a tremendous influence on the type of manager that is required. The manager of a large farm has some skills that are very different and some skills that are similar to the manager of an aircraft factory

TABLE 2.9   Some of the more important direct factors influencing the action a manager should take

Factor	Action required to deal with factors
Changes in market	Find new market or develop new products appropriate to changed market conditions
Availability of supplies	Obtain supplies required from different suppliers who can provide the required quality cheaper. Modify operation so that different, less expensive supplies can be used
Availability of adequate finance	Ensure that finance is available to cover planned operations and all foreseeable contingencies
Staff adequacy in dealing with demands	If staff is not adequate arrangements must be made to either recruit appropriate staff or retrain existing staff so that they can deal with future requirements effectively
Production facilities inadequate. (Production facilities may be a factory, office, laboratory, farm, school or hospital)	Ensure that production facilities, no matter what form they take, are appropriate to current and future needs. It is vital that production facilities are equal to and if possible better than competitors.
Organisation's long-term needs	This is a very difficult factor to deal with as the long-term future is by its very nature uncertain. However, it is prudent to make some provision for the long-term needs

TABLE 2.10 Some of the more important indirect factors influencing the action a manager can take

Factor	Action required to deal with factors
National political factors	Monitor and carefully assess political statements about future legislation and government policy. Rarely will political changes take place quickly – the time-scale is likely to be years
International political factors	Influence of international political factors is more difficult to interpret than national factors. It may be some governments are at war or some countries are in slump conditions that have an adverse effect on trade
Pressure group action including pressure from the media	Pressure group action takes many forms from strikes and demonstrations to control of the media to sponsoring election programmes of those favourable to their views. Their potential impact must be assessed and appropriate action taken to deal with their potential impact
Socio-political pressures – such as union demands	Socio-political pressures can be considered as just a part of pressure group activity. Such pressures can lead to changes in demand, which may result in a demand for certain products changing dramatically
Fashion	Fashion does not just apply to dresses, it applies to most manufactured goods. In some cases it might just be called taking account of technical developments. Manufacturers have to monitor trends and make sure that their products satisfy current fashions
Government stability	If a country's government is not stable it is likely that the country's economy will be weak and demand will be low. Larger companies will look for other markets. Small companies are unlikely to have the flexibility to move and will just have to accept some refreshment.

This brief examination of indirect factors shows how inherently unpredictable they are, and at the same time how difficult it is for a manager to predict their impact. The difficulty is no excuse for a manager neglecting any one of these factors. A manager must find some way of identifying the impact of the factors on his/her short-term and long-term plans. The first predictions of the impact of problem factors are likely to have a very large margin of error associated with them, but as time goes by better information becomes available and the margins of error are likely to be smaller.

There is of course an element of a gamble in deciding what action has to be taken and the prudent manager will make provision for dealing with every adverse condition he/she can identify. Being able to deal with adverse conditions in the long term is likely to make a company that is able to survive the difficulties and grow and prosper.

Conclusions

Not all managers are the same, some have just routine functions while others have wide responsibilities and are involved not only in ensuring current requirements are satisfied but that the organisation continues to develop. This chapter has concentrated on management in the wider sense in the belief that good management must always devote some effort to planning how to deal with future developments, and determining the acceptability of the risks associated with an organisation's activities. Risk assessment and management are two functions shared with all entrepreneurs.

Eleven skills were identified as characterising the essential capability good managers require. The 11 skills are:

1   Negotiating

2   Planning

3   Risk assessment and management

4   Purchasing

5   Accounting

6   Recruitment

7   Training

8   Selling

9   Ensuring that controls are satisfied

10   Dealing with emergencies

11   Capability for dealing with elected members

In practice the weight a particular manager decides to give to each factor depends on the specific role defined for the manager, the type and size of the organisation involved. The most successful and effective organisations are likely to have managers that understand all aspects of the organisation and can perform many of the tasks involved. Such managers generally command considerable respect from those they manage, as they are seen to have a real understanding of the problems to be dealt with, such as those associated with emergencies, introducing change and adapting to future needs.

In planning the future of an organisation a manager must be aware of nine types of problem and the uncertainties associated with their solution. The nine types of problem are:

1 Identification of the risks involved

2 Human resources shortages

3 Equipment out of date

4 Material supply difficulties

5 Wars/riots changing demand and way of life

6 Government policy changing pattern of demands and supplies

7 Finance availablity

8 Client/customer relations – can they be improved to the company's advantage?

9 Climate – will it interfere with operations?

The two case studies considered showed the benefits of developing both short-term and long-term plans for bringing a project to a successful conclusion.

It was also recognised that a successful manager has to understand both the direct and indirect factors that condition the environment he/she has to operate in. Six important indirect factors that condition the operational environment were identified as being:

1 National political factors

2 International political factors

3 Pressure group action, including pressure from the media

4 Socio-political pressures such as union demands

5 Fashion

6 Government stability

Because of the variable nature of the indirect factors they are very difficult to make precise allowance for. The best a manager can do is to make informed judgements and to monitor the situation, responding to changes in the situation as they occur. It is accepted that some modelling techniques and Bayesian-related methods can help the decision making.

The direct factors, which may to some extent be influenced by indirect factors, are a little easier to deal with. Important among the direct factors managers must allow for are:

1   Changes in the market

2   Availability of supplies

3   Availability of adequate finance

4   Staff adequate to deal with demands

5   Production facilities adequate

6   Satisfaction of organisation's needs

References

'MoD to act on costs and delays' (1999) *Professional Engineering*, 7 July: 7.
'NHS managers warned on PFI cost overruns' (1999) *The New Civil Engineer*, 9 September: 8.

CHAPTER THREE

The forms of entrepreneurism

The concept of entrepreneurism is simple, it is the heart of exploiting an activity or business for profit. In general it is taken that the profit is measured in money terms. However, there are many cases where it is not possible to measure profit precisely in money terms. Major cases where it is difficult to measure profit/benefit directly in money terms include: the benefit of the armed forces, the benefit of medical treatment and the value of the social services. The problem of assessing the value of activities that cannot be measured directly in money terms does to some extent destroy the possibility of using conventional methods of cost-benefit analysis in a precise way.

Now to look more carefully at the characteristics of entrepreneurism in a range of activities. Table 3.1 gives a summary of the entrepreneurial characteristics in a sample of activities. From this very simplified view of the various types of entrepreneurism three main types emerge:

Type 1 All operations carried out in an open market.
Type 2 Some operations are funded or subsidised by government.
Type 3 Operations are entirely funded either by central or local government. Funding is subject to political decisions.

In practice there are many variations of the three main types of entrepreneurism. In some ways the hybrid type is more common than the pure type. Whatever the form of entrepreneurism it is a product of four main factors, demand, government influence, private sector influence and political influence. The proportion of particular factors varies with the type of entrepreneurism. Figure 3.1 shows diagrammatically how these factors may interact for a particular case. From the diagram it will be noticed that the supply factor is missing. This is because it is taken that the entrepreneur responds to demand by providing a supply to satisfy the demand. An important variation of this situation is where an entrepreneur identifies a new product and develops a market to absorb the supply of the new product. Examples of this approach are breech loading guns, personal computers and mobile telephones. In reality the list of new products that have led to new markets being created is enormous and it is assumed each reader will have their own pet list of new products that have created new markets. The influence of individual factors varies tremendously from case to case. In some cases market conditions may dominate, in other cases political influences may dominate.

It is important to remember that where political influences dominate, at least part of the costs involved is likely to be borne by government, which ultimately draws the required funds from taxpayers.

There are also other important variables in entrepreneurism:

1   The size of the operation

2   The country in which the activity is carried out

FIGURE 3.1   Diagrammatic representation showing how the main factors involved interact to produce a particular type of entrepreneurism

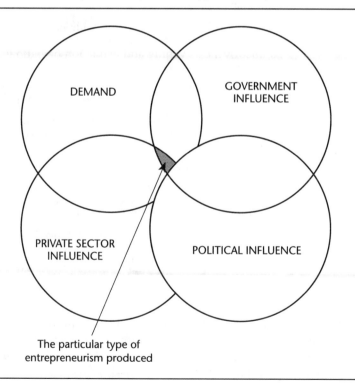

The particular type of
entrepreneurism produced

TABLE 3.1   Summary of the entrepreneurial characteristics of a range of activities

Activity	Entrepreneurial characteristics
Armed forces	Depends on government funding, has to live within the constraints of government policy. Has to demonstrate need for funding to satisfy criteria as an effective force in current circumstances. Purchasing services and equipment might be done on a commercial basis
Financial services (banking and insurance)	Must sell their products and buy their resources on the commercial market – subject to some government regulation
Manufacturing industries	Must sell their products and buy their resources on the commercial market – subject to some government regulation
Transport	Market for their products open but subject to some national and international government regulations. Market for resources open, but limited to the extent that supply is dominated by a few major suppliers
Agriculture	Large part of the market for the products subject to national and international subsidy. Government action can influence market, e.g. reaction to BSE in beef, salmonella in eggs
Mining	Trade in an international market, wide range of mining and extraction conditions influence price and competitiveness. Mining and extraction operations subject to state regulation
Fishing	Size of catches regulated by international agreement. Some subsidies for laying up boats and building new ones
Hotels	Fairly open market – some government regulation of food hygiene and working conditions. Have to show a profit to survive
Media	Open market – has to show a profit to survive.
Civil service	Does not have to show a profit on its operations but has to justify its need for funding. Activities dictated by government and codified in legislation
Local government	Does not have to show a profit but has to justify to central government its funding requirements. Operations regulated by government and defined by legislation

Table 3.2 summarises the influences of size on the nature of entrepreneurism. Table 3.3 summarises the influences of a country on the nature of entrepreneurism and Table 3.4 summarises the various levels of entrepreneurial responsibility that may exist in an organisation.

TABLE 3.2   The influence of size on the nature of entrepreneurism

Size	Typcial inflence on the nature of entrepreneurism
Small (less than 100 employees)	Depends to a large extent on local market conditions or for a government type of organisation on very limited terms of reference. Too small to influence national or international markets
Medium (100–1000 employees)	May be involved nationally and internationally. In some cases where a very special product or service is involved might operate as a monopoly
Large national company (1000–10,000 employees)	Likely to be involved both nationally or internationally and could have a controlling influence in the market
Large international (10,000–100,000 or more employees)	Dominant position in the world market. Should be strong enough to increase its influence in the market. Examples of such organisations are: Ford, General Motors, General Electric, Glaxo, L'Oreal, Boeing, Novartis, Unilever, Esso and in the political arm NATO, The European Commission and the UN

TABLE 3.3   The influence of type of country on the nature of entrepreneurism

Country	Characteristics of government and business
Free market (Developed country democratic government)	Market forces determines price and volume. Producers have to respond to market forces. Government influence kept to a minimum. Corruption level likely to be low
Free market (Developing country developed government)	Market forces determine price and volume. Government and currency may not be stable. Corruption level likely to be higher than in a developed country
Restricted market (Democratic govern-ment developed country)	Price and volume determined by regulation. Considerable variation possible over time. Government may not be stable. Some corruption expected.
Restricted market (Dictatorship developed country)	Price and volume limited by regulation. Over time limited variation allowed but controlled. Life of government limited to life of dictator. Some corruption expected
Restricted market (Dictatorship developing country)	Price and volume limited by regulation. Considerable variation possible over time. Currency and government may not be stable. Radical change when dictator no longer in power. Some corruption to be allowed for

TABLE 3.4   Summary of the levels of entrepreneurism that may exist in an organisation

Level of entrepreneurism*	Scope	Examples
1	Comprehensive responsibility for all aspects of operations in a free market situation	Owner or chief executive of organisation. If a large organisation is involved he/she would have support staff
2	Single function entrepreneur	The person involved may just be involved with selling or purchasing. The single function may be recruiting staff where the concern will be getting the required staff at the best price
3	Function defined by legislation	This would be a civil service department where the concern is to perform the department function as efficiently as possible
4	Voluntary organisation running a charitable organisation	Religious organisation, club, professional society. Although not strictly commercial there will be entrepreneurial activity to the extent that they want to obtain sufficient funds to support their activities.

* Note: 1 is the highest level of entrepreneurism

Each type of entrepreneurism can be characterised by three factors, which are size, market condition and form of government. These characteristics can be considered to form a three-dimensional matrix as shown in Figure 3.2. The rating could be interpreted as giving a measure of the risk associated with an activity, this topic will be returned to in Chapter 9 and Appendix 3. The three-digit description of entrepreneurial characteristics gives size, market condition, and form of government. For example, an activity with a 1.3.2 rating would be an activity in a free market rating 1, with an organisation size over 1000 employees giving a rating of 3 and a partly dictatorial form of government giving a rating 2.

It could be argued that a three-dimensional description is a gross oversimplification of the characteristics of any form of entrepreneurial activity. However, it does provide a starting point for investigating the

FIGURE 3.2 Matrix of functions defining entrepreneurial characteristics

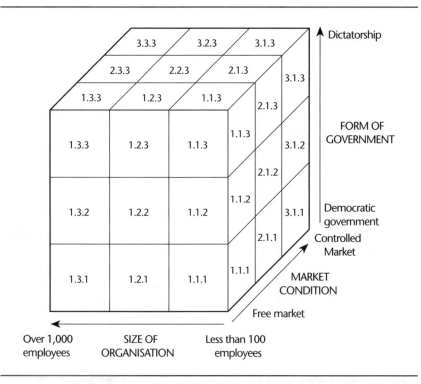

characteristics. To illustrate just how complex the spectrum of character-istics can be, two examples are considered, one from the private sector and the other from the public sector. The private sector example is an aircraft company and the public sector example is a county council.

The private sector example is an aircraft company that currently and in the immediate past has been making military aeroplanes for its own government. The market is open to the extent that when new orders are placed tenders from abroad are considered. Also when there is a chance of an order from abroad the government might give the company a grant which would help it make its bid for the order more competitive. If the government has a special relationship with the foreign country it might exert some form of pressure that would make the bid from abroad more acceptable. So the market does not fit exactly the description of a free market, it could be more accurately described as a politically pressurised free market.

The size characteristic of the company is equally complex. It is not just size alone, it is also capability. Has the company the capability to take on new novel work and has it the resources to expand? It could be that design and research teams have been run down and the size of the company's resources reduced.

This could cause a problem, as the next generation of aeroplane is likely to require a larger team with a more advanced range of skills. If the company is not able to expand its design and research capability it would not be given consideration as the designer of a new series of aeroplanes. The question of developing suitable strategies is discussed in more detail in Chicken and Hayns (1999).

The political environment in which a company has to operate also has a profound effect on the way it operates. At one extreme everything the company does may be controlled by a dictatorial government. The government may dictate what the company does or makes and the government may dictate the price at which the company sells its products. At the other end of the spectrum the company may be quite free to decide what it makes and the price at which it sells its product.

For all organisations there is a plethora of government regulations that must be satisfied. The regulations include: tax, health and safety, working time, environment pollution, the responsibilities of directors. So a company operating in a free market is not entirely free, there are always some regulations that have to be satisfied. Some of the regulations may be national and some may be international. Regulations such as those adapted by the European Union are examples of international regulations. The role of regulation is discussed further in Chapter 5.

A public body like a county council has many of the entrepreneurial characteristics of any public body and illustrates well the complexity of these characteristics. Looking at the characteristics in the same order as the characteristics of a private company and starting with the market, for a public body it could be said that their operations are controlled by a form of dictatorship. They have to operate within budget constraints imposed on them by central government.

A controlled budget means that a council can only undertake the range of activities it can pay for within its budget restrictions. It is of course possible to shuffle the range of activities funded so that the range of activities includes some of those of special interest to the elected council.

Although entrepreneurial activity is very different between the public and private sectors and generally it is considered entrepreneurism is a unique feature of the private sector, there are some interesting and important aspects of entrepreneurism employed in the public sector. The most important applications of entrepreneurism are those associated with purchasing and placing contracts. In placing contracts the public sector assess tenders in very much the same way an organisation in the private sector does. Their method of assessment of tender has to be transparent as they may be subject to audit.

In calling for tenders in both the public and the private sectors the tender process consists of five main steps:

1   Define the project that is to be the subject of the tender.

2   Prepare a detailed design. The more precisely the project is designed the less chance there is of misunderstandings.

3   Prepare a call for tenders setting out exactly what has to be and what has not to be included in the tender.

4   Assess the acceptability of the tender. The assessment to include evaluation of the tenderer's capability and financial soundness.

5   Plan to place the contract with the lowest bidder but if the lowest tender is not for some reason acceptable the reasons must be sound and defensible.

In the public sector besides contracts for the supply of goods there have been some interesting developments in the way public sector organisations are allowed to operate. Some of the developments involve a very comprehensive application of the basic tenets of entrepreneurism. The main thrust of these developments has been the privatisation of public sector organisations and attempts to improve public sector efficacy by forming partnerships. Among the forms that this exploitation of entrepreneurism has taken are:

1   Whole units of the central and local government organisation have passed to private industry to operate. This type of privatisation has often taken the form of a unit/department being taken over by a contractor and the authority involved having to buy the service from the contractor. In such cases the contractor often initially takes over the existing staff of the unit/department involved but injects its own managers and gives them the responsibility of improving operational efficiency. This may involve getting rid of staff who do not produce the required level of performance.

2   Sometimes partnerships are formed with other similar organisations. These partnerships may take the form of two or more local authorities' units operating in the same area and performing similar tasks joining forces to form a more effective unit. Such a partnership may be formed to bring together road maintenance units from a district and county council. Generally existing staff would be used

to make up the partnership teams. When such units are formed some staff might prefer not to be involved and take redundancy rather than get involved in a new venture. The resulting changes in the team may improve efficiency.

Another important type of partnership that is used is where a department forms a partnership with a contractor to undertake a particular contract. In such partnerships the department usually controls expenditure and the contractor provides the workforce and equipment. In some forms of such partnerships both parties provide funding, the department providing funding directly in money terms and the contractor providing funding in kind. The department/contractor type of partnership is used for defence and transport type projects.

From the description of entrepreneurism so far it is clear there are many levels of entrepreneurism in society. The range includes: those just involved with purchasing, those just concerned with selling and those with comprehensive responsibility for purchasing, selling and development of the organisation. The level of entrepreneurism is in many ways related to the level of management responsibility involved. I stress that I do not wish to give the impression that I believe every organisation has to have a complicated hierarchical structure. I recognise that most organisations have to perform many functions, but complex management systems of the various functions can lead to inefficiency. In large complex management systems many people can become so isolated from the real foundation of decision making that they lose sight of or interest in the real aims of the organisation.

The first point I wish to make about entrepreneurism at this stage is that it is an ever-changing dynamic situation. The managers/decision makers must be prepared to react to changes in the entrepreneurial environment in a flexible yet positive way. It has to be recognised that decisions will often have to be based on qualitative evidence or models. Such evidence is by its very nature flawed and the decision has to allow for surprises in the difference between the predictions of the model and what happens in the real world. The further into the future models predict the greater uncertainty has to be allowed for. Also with qualitative data even the shape of the distribution associated with such data is unknown.

It has been suggested (Hammitt and Shiyakhter 1999) that even in the measurements of fundamental physical constants new data can have standard deviations considerably greater than the old. This helps to put into perspective the uncertainties that must be allowed for in qualitative predictions of circumstances 10 to 20 years ahead. The uncertainty also varies with the type of activity. It has also been suggested there should be a 'Surprise Index' to give an indication of how much new data differs from previous estimates.

Another way of looking for surprises in data is to look for outliers in the data. One useful method for doing this is the Dixon method described in Chicken (1996).

Conclusions

It has been shown that there are three main forms of entrepreneurism:

1   Open market conditions

2   Conditions when operations are partly funded or subsidised by government

3   Conditions when operations are fully funded by government

It is recognised that in a large organisation there are likely to be people with various levels of entrepreneurial responsibility. These levels are described in Table 3.4.

The form of entreprenerism is also influenced by the size of the operation involved and the country in which the activity has to be carried out. It is important to recognise the influence of socio-political factors on entrepreneurism. The list of socio-political factors that influence entrepreneurism is long and includes:

1   political parties' aims

2   legislation including planning approval, subsidies, health and safety, environment regulation, working hours and company regulation.

A way of coding the character of the various forms of entrepreneurism is proposed which rates the three main characteristics of entrepreneurism on a three-point scale. The three characteristics rated are: market conditions, size of organisation involved and form of government. The rating system would rate an organisation working in a free market as 1, with about 750 employees as 2 and operating in a dictatorship would be rated 3. This would give the overall rating of 1.2.3.

References

Chicken, J.C. and Hayns, M.R. (1999) *Strategy and Priority*, London: Thomson Business Press.

Hammitt, J.K. and Shiyakhter, A.I. (1999) 'The expected value of information and the probability of surprise', *Risk Analysis* 19(1), February: 136.

Chicken, J.C. (1996) *The Risk Handbook*, London: Thompson International Press.

▪ CHAPTER FOUR ▪

The forms of management

Management takes many forms, some effective in some circumstances and others effective in other circumstances. There are of course those forms of management that are not effective in any circumstances and can lead to the decay or even death of an organisation. The main factors that determine the form of management can be considered as a matrix, a simple form of which is shown in Table 4.1.

In making an assessment of the efficacy of the various forms of management it is important to maintain a vigorous sense of humour. One important writer that did much to develop an appropriate humorous and at the same time critical outlook on management was the late Professor Parkinson. (Professor Parkinson's Law that work expands so as to fill the time available for its completion was published in 1958 under the title *Parkinson's Law: The Pursuit of Progress*. The book has been regarded as the

TABLE 4.1 A simple matrix of the factors that determine the form of management

Type	Size	
	Large	*Small*
Public body	State industry	District council
	Civil service department	A small outpost of a government department
Private industry	Multinational manufacturing company	A small consultancy operated by 2–5 people
	A bank	A small shop in a country district

first humorous book about the science of office management to be a best seller). I know how much it has influenced my own thinking about the characteristics of various forms of management. I also know how perceptive his observations were recognised to be.

In my own view the most successful forms of management are those in which the managers have a detailed understanding of all the processes involved. It follows almost directly from that statement that the least successful forms of management are those where the manager hides behind a mahogany desk and considers it vital to avoid being involved directly in the working processes involved. These characteristics are illustrated particularly well in the contrast between a successful one-person business and a civil service department. The one-person business is run by an active person understanding and being competent in all aspects of his/her business and aiming to expand the business. The characteristics of the mahogany desk syndrome are found in organisations with a Parkinson's Law type of approach to their work. It is recognised that the problems may not be due to individual managers but imposed on them by the people setting up the organisation.

Two central questions about forms of management are: (1) What are the characteristics important to successful management exhibited by the small business? (2) What are the damaging characteristics of the mahogany desk syndrome? The characteristics summarised in Table 4.2 represent a gross simplification of the real world, but they serve as the starting point for the discussion as follows.

The first essential of an effective management organisation is that it must have clearly defined aims. Without well-defined aims management activities are likely to drift and dissolve into a mass of non-productive and self-perpetuating activities. One manifestation of the development of

TABLE 4.2 Important characteristics of management schemes

Type of management	Type of characteristic
Small successful business	Management objective is staying in business and improving business management. They know every detail of the business
An organisation where the management has the mahogany desk syndrome	Management more concerned with maintaining personal position than developing the organisation. They leave the real decisions about vital details to others

such a negative approach to management is often growth in non-productive committees and meetings that feel no real responsibility for having a useful output. Generally proliferation of committees and meetings means someone or some part of an organisation does not have staff with the right skills or training or is unwilling to take responsibility. It is recognised that some committees and meetings can help communication between different sections of an organisation, but with good management the need for committees and meetings is kept to a minimum. Table 4.3 summarises some of the aims that may be set for managers.

Now to look more closely at the forms of management that exist in the real world. It is often convenient to categorise management types according to the industry they are associated with. Table 4.4 presents a summary of the main types of management and includes military/police activities. From Table 4.4 it is clear that in each case, even including military/police activities, the basic actions required are:

1 Identify what is needed or has to be done.

2 Organise the resources.

3 Monitor performance and make sure the task is completed.

4 Plan ahead (future requirements).

5 Deal with any problems that arise.

For each activity every element will have its own special technical characteristics. The activities required to make a car engine are rather different from the activities required to complete a surgical operation.

TABLE 4.3   Some aims set for management

Management aims set for an active commercial organisation	Management aims set for civil service type organisations
1. Increase sales	1. Keep expenditure within funding
2. Improve product designs	2. Control service products
3. Increase production	3. Implement legislation
4. Monitor staff performance	4. Monitor staff performance
5. Train staff	5. Train staff
6. Recruit staff	6. Recruit staff
7. Select contractors	7. Select contractors

TABLE 4.4 The main categories of management type

Industry	Management characteristics
Manufacturing	Concerned with organising the resources for design, production and sale
Transport/travel	Concerned with organising the means of transport, finding the customers and completing the travel required
Agriculture	Assessing what products are going to be required and producing them. Often small teams, seasonal variation in work.
Banking and financial services	Identifying what loans, insurance and investments will be required. Designing suitable products and marketing them. Also ensuring that adequate funds will be available
Retail business	Determining what products will be required in six months' time and obtaining suitable supplies, then selling them
Media	Producing products such as: films, radio/TV programmes, videos and newspapers that are likely to be of interest to the public
Medicine/dentistry	Identifying the medical and dental problems the public has and dealing with them in a helpful way
Military/police	Strict discipline following orders that are hard to complete. Management structure withdrawn. Success generally depends on team spirit
Hotels/restaurants	Ensure guests are satisfied, supplies are delivered on time and of the required quality, ensure facilities are utilised as fully as possible and that they are maintained in good order

Both activities will fail unless all the people involved are motivated to carry out activities effectively. It is possible to believe the people involved in making car engines might conceivably be retrained to carry out surgical operations, but the amount of retraining would be enormous. The technical know-how required to manage a particular activity is one of the main differences between managers in different industries.

In organisations where there is no factory-like physical output, it can be difficult to measure efficiency or performance. One approach that can be helpful, if it is used consistently, is the Personal Achievement and Development Scheme (PADS). The essentials of the PADS procedure are:

1   Staff member is subject to a regular structured confidential interview by his/her line manager.

2   At the interview the staff member is asked to identify:

   i)   What contribution he/she has made to an organisation's activities

   ii) How the contribution could be improved

   iii) What additional training would help improve performance

3   At the end of the interview a programme of actions to improve performance will be agreed between the member of staff and his/her line manager.

4   It is the line manager's job to ensure that the programme of actions is implemented.

It may be that one outcome of the PADS review process is that the member of staff interviewed is found to be unsuitable for his or her present job and that another type of work has to be found for that person.

One activity that is common to both public bodies and private industry is selecting contractors. Mistakes in the selection of a contractor can seriously damage an organisation, it can even bankrupt a company.

The process of assessing a potential contractor's acceptability requires collection and evaluation of a great deal of data about the organisation. The data must be assessed in a logical and consistent way. Among the questions that must be asked are: financial status, previous experience with the contractor, contractor's experience and competence in the supply of the goods or services of interest. It is also normal practice to check references, although references given by the contractor may be just those biased in the contractor's favour. Some of the questions that may be asked of a referee are identified in Table 4.5.

There is generally an enormous mass of data available about contractors. Assessment of such a mass of data is not an exact science and usually involves many subjective judgements. The risk ranking technique can be adapted to structure the assessment of such a mass of data in a logical way.

The five essential steps in any ranking process are:

1   Decide what has to be assessed.

2   Collect the relevant data/evidence.

3   Design the criteria for ranking the acceptability of the proposal.

TABLE 4.5 Examples of the questions that may be asked of a referee

PLEASE GIVE DETAILS OF THE MOST RECENT WORK THE CONTRACTOR DID FOR YOU		
Description of Work	Dates	Value

Please answer the two questions below:

	YES	NO
Was this company's approach to health and safety acceptable?		

If the opportunity arose would you employ this contractor again?		

PLEASE INDICATE THE LEVEL OF PERFORMANCE SHOWN BY THIS CONTRACTOR IN EACH AREA OF WORK BELOW				
Keeping delivery promises	Very Good	Good	Adequate	Poor
	Comments:			
Satisfactory quality and specification	Very Good	Good	Adequate	Poor
	Comments:			
Price adjustment	Very Good	Good	Adequate	Poor
	Comments:			
Overall feelings about how the contract went	Comments:			

4   Using the ranking criteria determine on the basis of the data/ evidence available what ranking the acceptability of the proposal justifies.

5   On the basis of the ranking make a decision about the acceptability of the proposition being considered.

In rating and weighting the acceptability of any activity there are a number of important implications management has to be consider. The problem is centred on the possibility that the weighting process distorts the value of some of the factors considered. This problem is first illustrated by means of an example and then the overall strategy for assessing complex proposals/projects is examined.

The example considered is the assessment of potential contractors to provide a service in various countries, the service being to promote interests in various countries in exploiting the client's high technology services and products, and the client being a government agency. The potential contractors are expected initially to fund half the cost of providing the service and then in the long term to make a profit from the commission they earn on the contracts they negotiate for the exploitation of the client's high technology.

The potential contractors are advised that their proposal will be assessed on five aspects:

1   The appropriateness of their proposed approach, methodology and work plan.

2   The potential of the proposed approach for improving the client's commercial exploitation of its high technology portfolio.

3   The adequacy of their management organisation and resources.

4   The contribution that the contractor's work is likely to make to the economic wellbeing of the client.

5   The contribution that the contractor's work would make to the quality of the client's socio-political environment.

First thoughts were that the individual factors should be assessed on a 1 to 5 scale with the rating being in whole numbers and allocated in the following way:

1   Equals a poor predicted performance

2   Equals a fair predicted performance

3   Equals an average predicted performance

4   Equals a good predicted performance

5   Equals an excellent predicted performance

If each aspect was considered excellent the overall score would be 25, and if each aspect was considered to be poor the overall score would be 5. The overall score for other combinations of score would be somewhere between 5 and 25.

There are two problems with this scoring system:

1   With an odd number of rating ranks it is possible the assessor would be neutral in his/her assessment and would tend to overuse the mid-ranking. This would skew the basis for decision making.

2   Each factor was considered to be of equal importance as implied by the linear system of rating.

With the first problem the solution would be to reduce the steps in the rating scale to four. This would give two ratings that were broadly unacceptable and two ratings that were acceptable. The middle neutral/ negative rating would disappear.

The solution to the second problem is not so easy and depends to a large extent on the client's priorities. Even the best advice about the ratio of importance is likely to be subjective. But how they are arrived at must, for good management, be transparent. Also the rating system must be such that bad ratings cannot be obscured by good ratings. This last problem is generally easily settled by giving bad ratings a high numerical score and good ratings a low score.

One solution that has been found to give acceptable results is the 1, 2 , 5, 14 scale. The effectiveness of this scale has been demonstrated on several occasions (Chicken 1994, 1996). The merit of this scale is shown by the following example of the assessment of four proposals. The proposals are identified simply as proposal 1, 2, 5 and 14. The characteristics assessed are management, financial strength and technical quality of proposal. The management characteristic is taken to be a measure of the management structure and the competence of managers allocated to the project. The financial strength of the proposal is taken as a measure of the adequacy of the proposer's financial resources to deal with all the difficulties likely to arise in the course of bringing the project to fruition. In many ways assessing the financial strength of a proposer is like assessing the creditworthiness of a company. The technical quality of a proposal is a very broad term and is intended to include all the activities needed to bring a proposal to fruition that are not included in the other two headings.

The scoring process is summarised in Table 4.6. From the table it can be seen that proposal 4 is the most acceptable and proposal 2 the least acceptable. In practice building up a ranking of a proposal may involve many stages.

TABLE 4.6 Summary of the process of ranking the acceptability of proposals 1 to 4

Proposal	Factor score	Overall score	Conclusion
1	Management 5		Needs considerable modification to make acceptable
	Financial 5	12	
	Technical 2		Rank 3
2	Management 5		Unlikely it can be made acceptable
	Financial 5	24	
	Technical 14		Rank 4
3	Management 1		Can be made acceptable with slight modification
	Financial 1	4	
	Technical 2		Rank 2
4	Management 1		Acceptable without restriction
	Financial 1	3	
	Technical 1		Rank 1

Factor score scheme   14   = Unlikely to be acceptable

                       5   = Only acceptable if it can be modified considerably

                       2   = Only requires slight modification to make acceptable

                       1   = Likely to be acceptable without restriction

Overall score scheme 16–42 = Unlikely it can be made acceptable Rank 4

                    7–15 = Needs considerable modification to make acceptable Rank 3

                     4–6 = Acceptable needs slight modification Rank 2

                       3   = Acceptable without restriction Rank 1

Although a proposal may be rated highly before work starts it may be that what is produced in practice is not up to the standards promised. This fact alone underlines the importance of careful monitoring of a project from the moment it is initiated until it is operating effectively. Such monitoring is an essential management control.

If for some reason effective monitoring cannot take place there is a very high risk the project/proposal will not be completed on time or within budget or satisfy its operational specification. Careful monitoring of work is a fundamental function of management. It is not a responsibility that management can shirk, the job has to be done and done with staff that have the appropriate competence. If the client does not have such staff they must be recruited or hired in some other way. Hiring staff on a short-term basis often brings in its train other problems, such as hired staff not being familiar with a client's organisation and lines of communication not being effective. It is of course management's responsibility to ensure that these problems are minimised.

For a major proposal there are likely to be many stages in the assessment. The components to be assessed at each stage are rated on the basis of three characteristics such as demand, financial and technical. The structure of a major assessment is outlined in Figure 4.1. The starting point is a mass of information which has to be distilled to give an overall assessment of acceptability. At each stage the number of components to be considered is iteratively reduced. The multi-stage multivariable approach to assessment really represents a progressive weighting of the significance of the factors considered and to a large extent eliminates possible bias in the final stage of assessment.

In the early stages of an assessment the factors rated are likely to be different at each stage and must be adjusted to suit the specific nature of the project/proposal being considered. Whatever rating factors are adopted they must be used in a consistent and transparent way so that assessments are generally comparable.

Rating factors that may be appropriate include: cost, availability, proved suitability, adequacy for performance, socially/politically acceptable, amount of research/development required, acceptably safe, environmentally safe, through life net benefit.

It is stressed the list is not comprehensive and the rating factors used must be carefully selected to be appropriate to the situation involved. It is recognised that some factors are of little significance and can be neglected, but it should be clearly recorded that their neglect is considered to be justified.

The process of building up a comprehensive assessment of proposal/ project can be appreciated by considering the following example. A

FIGURE 4.1 Outline of the structure of a major assessment

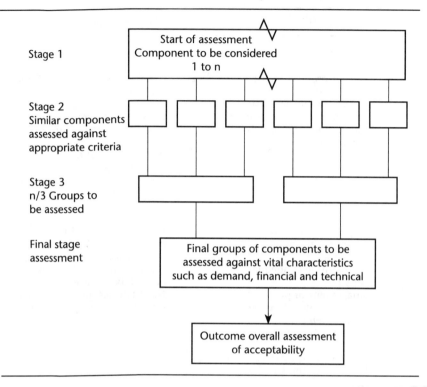

government department has asked for proposals to modernise all state schools in a specific area. It has been specified that the proposals should be based on some form of private finance initiative. The assessment can be considered from two perspectives, which are the perspective of the client and the perspective of the proposer/contractor. In both cases the range of factors to be considered is similar but the interpretation is different. Table 4.7 shows something of the nature of the differences in the two perspectives. The client will be more concerned with establishing there is a need for the proposal/project and the contractor is more concerned with undertaking the work, making a profit and being paid on time.

It is important to note that the assessment should consider the whole spectrum of possible values. The basic assessment will be based on nominal values of the data involved but in addition the upper and lower limits of the values involved have to be considered. In practical terms this means three assessments have to be made: the assessment based on the nominal values of data and assessments based on the upper and lower level values of data.

TABLE 4.7   Differences in perspective in assessing acceptability

Client	*Proposer (contractor)*
Factors considered	Factors considered
Stage 1 Need for proposal/project Overall cost Specification to be satisfied (work to be done on schools) Arranging for appropriate funds to be available	Stage 1 Capability to satisfy specification Is it possible to arrange to fund the proposal in some way that does not involve the client directly in the funding? Will there be an adequate profit margin in such an arrangement? Are resources available to satisfy specification on required time- scales?
Stage 2 Adequate funding available, perhaps via proposer/ contractor Proposal/project adequately defined Management of proposal/ project clearly defined and client's interests and responsibilities effectively protected Prepare call for tenders Identify how tenders will be assessed	Stage 2 Decide if there is likely to be a benefit in making a bid. Develop an appropriate bid, and identify any problems that may have to be dealt with. Negotiate acceptance of the bid, including method of funding
Stage 3 Management of proposal/ Final project satisfactory Stage Financial arrangements satisfactory (funds available to meet all contingencies) Solutions to all technical problems available	Stage 3 Management of proposal/ Final project satisfactory from Stage proposer/contractor's point of view. Financial resources and arrangement satisfactory including prompt payment of bills. Solution of all technical problems within the capability and competence of the proposor/contractor

The process outlined for assessing the acceptability of a complex proposal can be summarised in the following way:

1   Identify the factors that have to be assessed at each stage in the life of a proposal project. Also note those factors that it is considered to be justified to neglect.

2   Assess the acceptability of the various factors stage by stage. This means that only the factors relevant to a particular stage are assessed at that stage.

3   Make the assessment for the nominal upper and lower limit of all the factors involved.

4   Ranking scale used should be a simple four-point scale such as 1, 2, 5 and 14 so that an adverse score cannot be obscured by a good score.

5   Care should be taken only to include in the analysis factors of similar importance. It is misleading to try to combine the analysis of significant factors with those of little significance. In a large project there may be many minor factors that taken together have major significance. In such cases the minor factors may be combined so that they may be considered as one large factor equal in significance to the other large factors. It is of course important to establish just what the significance of the combined factor is.

A simple form of the ranking of the acceptability of potential contractors is summarised in Tables 4.8 and 4.9. For a real life case the factors assessed have to be adjusted to the type of contractor being considered. It is quite irrelevant to ask a clothing manufacturer questions about site conditions and to ask a construction firm questions about styling. Table 4.8 shows the type of factors that might be assessed for an engineering component manufacturer. The rank scoring scale shown is designed so that unacceptable assessment of one factor cannot be masked by good assessments of other factors.

Table 4.9 shows the conclusions that can be drawn from the total ranking scores of the factors considered.

For a major project, because of the enormous amount of detail that has to be evaluated, there may have to be many stages in building up the overall ranking of acceptability. In Figure 4.2 the iterative process of building up a ranking of acceptability for a major project is shown in a simplified form. The final assessment is built up from the assessment of all the individual components of every factor involved. The comprehensive assessment should include all the technical, economic and socio-political issues involved.

So far, the factors that determine the form of management required, the types of activity that have to be managed and some of the tools of management have been considered. The next step in the examination of forms of management is to consider four real life management situations to show how managers should behave and the fault situations that may develop.

TABLE 4.8 Factors to be assessed

Factor	Ranking feature	Ranking score
Financial strength	Sound financially	1
	Reported to be slow paying bills (usually a sign of financial weakness)	2
	Known to be under investigation by DTI	5
	Banks foreclosing on loans	14
Supply performance	Previous experience showed delivery on schedule and quality good	1
	High proportion of defective components delivered	2
	Delivery late with some defective parts	5
	Delivery late and quality unacceptable	14
References	All references asked for given and satisfactory	1
	Not all references asked for given but those given satisfactory	2
	References given critical of company involved	5
	No references given	14

TABLE 4.9 Conclusion justified by various ranking scores

Total ranking score	Conclusion justified
3	Company acceptable without reservations
4–6	Generally acceptable but some features of the company's performance will have to be monitored
7–15	The company's performance doubtful. The company would have to show it would improve its performance before it is given a contract
16–42	The company is unacceptable

The four situations are:

1   An engineering project manager responsible to the board of a large specialist company for developing fuel systems for jet engined aircraft.

FIGURE 4.2   A simplified diagram of the process of ranking the acceptability of a major project

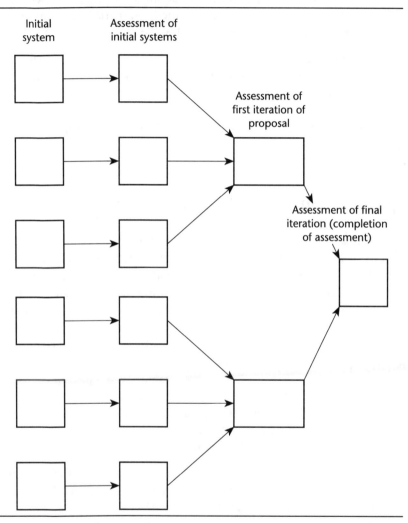

Note: In a real life case there are likely to be many more initial systems to be considered than shown in the diagram. It is important that the initial systems considered give a complete description of the proposition being evaluated. There may have to be many stages of iteration before a conclusion can be drawn.

2   The manager of a chemical factory which is one of several owned by a major international chemical company. Each factory has to operate as an independent profit centre.

3 A chief officer in a major county council. As chief officer he/she has overall responsibility for a staff of about 50 000. His/her freedom to operate is constrained by the council, legislation, central government and budgets fixed by central government.

4 A head of a civil service department in a major ministry. The range of action possible is set by legislation, government policy and employment practices agreed with the Unions.

The specification for each case is set out in the following specification sheets.

Specification case 1: fuel system project

The company makes a range of specialist fuel systems for jet engined aircraft; it holds many patents for such systems. In general the systems have to be tailored very carefully to match the performance of the aircraft for which it is intended. This tailoring involves design and a lot of testing of components and the whole system. The testing has to prove the system operates correctly at all the environmental conditions it will be exposed to in real life. Some of this testing will be carried out in a laboratory under simulated operational conditions and in real flight conditions.

The main board had accepted that the engineering project manager would have complete responsibility for bringing development of the fuel system for the A2 supersonic fighter bomber to a profitable conclusion.

The special features of this case are:

1 The main client for the project, the Ministry of Defence, only released contracts step by step. For example, a contract had been let for the conceptual design but no contract had been let for test or construction of a prototype or even a mock-up of the system.

2 This means the company has to build up the required technical teams with the risk that it may not get contracts for the next stage in the fuel system development.

3 There is a risk that the proposal to develop the A2 supersonic fighter bomber may be cancelled.

4 It is possible that some flight testing shows that at high altitudes the temperature is so low that the fuel freezes and blocks the main filters

and heaters have to be incorporated in the fuel system. Also at low temperatures the fuel flow meters become very inaccurate.

5   The company has to co-operate very closely with both the engine and the airframe designer as the details of engine and airframe design have a very large influence on the design of the fuel system. Initially relations between the fuel system, engine and airframe designers are somewhat strained due mainly to a personality conflict. As a matter of urgency the conflict has to be resolved.

Specification case 2: new chemical plant

The company makes a range of very special chemicals for which it holds many patents. In general to save distribution costs the company has the chemicals made near the demand centre. This means the production facilities are distributed around the world in factories owned and operated by subsidiary companies that act as profit centres. The profit centres are allowed to compete with each other to satisfy any particular demand.

The manager who has complete operational control of the subsidiary company has had his bid accepted to build and operate a new plant with a 10,000 ton/year capacity and cost of £25 million within five years. The subsidiary company has an appropriate site available, only a small engineering team and adequate financial reserves. The basic design of the plan will be provided by the company's Head Office, but the subsidiary company will have to increase its technical staff to do all the technical work required. It is also possible that consultants will have to be employed to help adapt the basic design to suit the subsidiary specific site.

The special features of this case are:

1   Tight financial and time-scale limits.

2   Shortage of skilled staff in the company.

3   Problems with the supply of very delicate components.

4   The demand might change reducing demand for the plant.

5   There may be considerable delays in getting all the planning approvals required.

Specification case 3: chief officer in a county council

The chief officer heads a very large organisation with staff in the region of 50 000. His/her responsibilities cover a very wide range: from schools to social services, from roads to planning approvals and from country parks to emergency services. The pressures a chief officer is under are equally diverse ranging from the public to local councils, from the government to the council elected members and from his own organisation to the media. The action a chief officer can take is constrained by legislation and the budget limitations fixed by the Treasury. Compliance with budget constraints are checked by the Government Auditor.

Some of the problems are compounded by the fact that many of the services previously considered to be unique to local government have been outsourced. This has resulted in local government losing staff and still having responsibility for ensuring the work is done correctly. Local government's role is that of the client and as such it has responsibility for ensuring that the work is done correctly and safely. There are ways of avoiding this responsibility such as giving another organisation comprehensive agency responsibility for the whole project. The contracts for such an agency agreement have to be drawn up very carefully which is a time-consuming process in itself.

The specific nature of the case that is considered in the following is the implementation of a government directive for local government to review the adequacy of the current stock of schools for the projected needs of the area over the next 20 years.

The special features of the case are:

1   Building a suitable team to make the review.

2   Setting the time-scale for the review.

3   Informing all the bodies that need to be aware of the review.

4   Collecting all the data required.

5   Determining the implication of the data.

6   Preparing a report on the review.

7   Agreeing with the relevant authorities how the finding of the review can be disseminated.

8   Determining if government policy will be adjusted to allow local authorities to adjust their building programmes to take account of the findings of the review.

Specification case 4: The head of a civil service department

The civil service department operates almost as an autonomous unit. Its function is defined by legislation. Its pay scales are fixed centrally, and leave very little scope for variation. Expenditure has to be kept strictly within the limits set by the Treasury.

The specific issue that the head of the department has to deal with is how savings can be made to allow his operational budget to be reduced over the following years by 10 per cent, that is by £150,000,000. The main function of the department is to purchase and store supplies for the Ministry of Defence.

The special features of the case are:

1   Determine what are the possible ways the required reduction in expenditure can be achieved.

2   Determine which method of achieving the required reduction in expenditure is likely to be the most efficient.

3   Determine which solution is most acceptable to his/her customer and to the department he/she has to report to.

4   Present the proposed solution to unions and staff organisations.

5   Implement the optimum solution.

The main question to be answered is how can the problem be solved in an acceptable way.

For each of the cases what seems to be the most acceptable solutions are now identified. Following examination of the possible solutions a number of general conclusions are drawn about what seems to be the essential messages about the optimum form of management for each of the four cases considered.

Analysis of management options

Case 1: fuel system project

The analysis of the management options is presented as a check list in Table 4.10, which identifies the action required and the form that the management action could take.

TABLE 4.10 Check list for the management action required for Case 1: fuel system project

Action required	Form that management action could take
Establish management structure required.	Determine the extent to which the manager wants to delegate responsibility and has staff to delegate responsibilities to.
Identify the technical description of the fuel system required.	This to a large extent will be dictated by the customer's specification but will have to be refined as the design proceeds and the results of testing become available.
Establish appropriate contact with customer.	This should be at the technical level as well as the commercial level.
Identify the time-scale.	Time-scales of interest are from concept to operation including maintenance.
Identify the funding available.	Availability of funding must be carefully linked with project time-scale and financial commitments.
Identify and make available the human resources required.	Resources committed must be matched with the availability of funding and time-scale for project.
Identify and make available the plant and equipment required.	Plant and equipment required must be available to match project time-scale and any difficulties with the availability of funding must be overcome.
Monitor progress towards completion of the job and that financial targets are being met.	The progress of the project must be monitored and action taken to solve any problems in achieving project targets or funding availability.
Identify action required beyond completion of projects.	Once the fuel systems are in service faults may develop with it that have to be solved. Also, there may be claims due to defective workmanship.

Central to the successful management of a project that is essentially for the supply of something to another contractor who is the main supplier to a client is maintaining close working relations between the two organisations. In the aerospace industry this is sometimes referred to as maintaining good supply chain relationships. The success of such a relationship depends on openness, honesty and trust between the parties involved. The success of the relationship should be monitored and any corrective action needed should be taken. One method of checking the success of the relationship is the Relationship Evaluation Tool (RET) which rates and weights the success characteristics of the various factors involved and builds up a success profile for the relationship. The parties involved have to agree what is an acceptable profile and make any changes to the relationship that have to be made to give it an acceptable profile.

The main conclusion drawn from this case is how important it is in a commercial situation for managers to maintain open, honest and trusting relations between suppliers and purchasers.

Case 2: new chemical plant

This case is to a very large extent an example of management in a free market situation. It is not quite a perfect free market situation. In the real world a perfect free market situation is unlikely to exist. In most markets there is some element of government involvement. The involvement can take many forms which include: taxation, health and safety requirements, constraints on imports and exports, subsidies, environment regulations and working time regulations.

Some decisions have been made, including: the capacity of the plant, the product that the plant is to produce and the date by which the plant has to be operational. Important among the decisions the manager still has to make are:

1   Is the detailed design of the plant and construction to be undertaken by the company's staff or by contractors? If by the company's staff additional staff will have to be recruited, but it is not clear that there will be work for them in five years.

2   An important question to be answered is how the company will manage contractors to ensure the plant built is to specification and timetable. (Some answers to this question must be settled before the tender stage.)

3   If consultants and construction contractors are employed the manager's concerns are how the costs will be kept within target and how the acceptability of the quality of the plant will be achieved.

4   Another concern about using contractors is that they obtain and may misuse commercially valuable information about how the chemical is produced.

5   How staff to operate the plant are to be obtained and trained.

TABLE 4.11 Decision options open to the manager in Case 2

Decision requirement	Possible options
Who undertakes design and construction.	1. All design and specifications to be provided by Head Office.
	2. Suitable team to be built up from suitable specialists available in other parts of the company.
	3. A complete new team to be recruited on the open market.
	4. Suitable contractors/consultants hired.
How is construction to be managed.	1. Appoint an outside company with appropriate skills to act as agent.
	2. Company to build up a suitable management team from its own staff.
	3. If contractors/consultants are used give them management responsibility, but they will need very precise instructions.
If contractors are used, how will costs targets and quality requirements be satisfied.	Whatever form of management is used clear targets have to be set. Incentives for keeping to targets include:
	1. Penalty for not achieving targets.
	2. Reward for achieving targets.
	3. Careful monitoring of progress and costs.
How is company-sensitive information to be protected.	1. Have all staff positively vetted (this means police records checked to see if they have been convicted of any crimes).
	2. Allowing access to any sensitive information only if certain passwords are known.
	3. Only letting carefully selected members of staff have access to the sensitive information.
	4. Give all staff security training.
How are staff to operate the plant to be obtained and trained.	1. From other companies in the group.
	2. By direct recruitment.
	3. By employing contractors/consultants.
	4. By appointing an agent to be responsible for the whole job.

Possible solutions to the above questions are given in Table 4.11. It may be that the manager will adopt a solution that will solve a combination of problem, the precise nature of the option adopted being tailored to the particular project involved.

Case 3: chief officer in a county council

The task of making an assessment of the adequacy of the county's stock of schools illustrates many of the managerial and entrepreneurial responsibilities of chief executives in local government. The task consists of eight parts:

1   Define the exact nature of the task to be undertaken.

2   Identify the staff required to make the assessment.

3   Obtain the staff required with the appropriate range of skills.

4   Assess the present stock of schools.

5   Determine how the required stock of schools has to be changed over the next 25 years due to demographic changes.

6   Determine the nature of the school demolition/construction programme for schools required over the next 25 years.

7   Prepare a report on the assessment.

8   Get council approval to submit the report to the government.

The chief officer will be concerned to staff the project in a way that will yield the quality of results that are expected within the budget requirements laid down. He will also be concerned that the results are politically acceptable both to his council and the government, so particular attention will be given to drafting the conclusions of the report and framing recommendations.

If as a result of the report the structure of the stock of schools requires dramatic changes, these changes in the stock will have implications that will have to be explained to staff and unions.

In the conventional way local government changes in the school stock do not involve the chief officer in making entrepreneurial-type decisions.

However, recent changes in the way public projects are financed does involve chief officers in taking a more commercial outlook. Two important variants of conventional practice that do involve chief officers taking a more commercial outlook are Design Build and Operate (DBO) contracts and Private Finance Initiative (PFI) contracts. In both cases the projects are, to a major extent, financed on a commercial basis by private industry, the difference being mainly in the contractual way private industry is compensated for by the county council.

In general central government has to agree the type of project that can be funded by PFI. At present experience with PFI-type contracts is somewhat limited. There is concern by the parties involved that there are not adequate allowances for or understanding of the risks that are borne by the various parties involved.

The main conclusion from this study of the role of a local government chief officer is that a chief officer's action is constrained by legislation and that he or she has to be sensitive to the political implications of their decisions and sensitive to the views of electoral members.

Case 4: head of a civil service department

The specific problem considered is the nature of the form of management the head of a civil service department has to use to reduce the budget by £150,000,000 in the following years. The main function of the department is to purchase supplies for the Ministry of Defence. This means that the bulk of the department's expenditure is paying for the purchase of supplies. The options that the head of the department has to consider are:

1   Reduce stocks and only purchase supplies when they are needed.

2   Agree with customer departments that they will reduce demands.

3   Find cheaper suppliers.

4   Reduce staff.

5   Dispose of assets (building, land) not essential to the future reduced role of the department.

Really the entrepreneurial element is rather one sided, it is just concerned with buying and selling at the best price. It is not concerned with developing markets. Essentially the action required is balancing the budget. There will be a lot of political infighting associated with all the possible solutions. It has to be recognised that none of the options open provides an instantaneous solution.

Conclusions

The overall conclusion about the forms of management available is that not all the forms are suitable for every application. The forms of management appropriate for a small private business are different to those needed for a large public body and the management required for private industry is different to that required for a civil service type of organisation.

Very important characteristics of all management roles are:

1   Defining what has to be done.

2   Assessing the options in a consistent way.

3   Obtaining the right human and financial resources.

4   Keeping good relations with customers and suppliers.

5   Making appropriate plans for the future.

6   Keeping promises about costs and deliveries.

References

Chicken, J.C. (1994) *Managing Risks and Decisions on Major Projects*, London: Chapman and Hall.
Chicken J.C. (1996) *Risk Handbook*, London: International Thomson Business Press.

CHAPTER FIVE

The real and imaginary constraints on management action

There are many constraints managements have to overcome to enable them to act in the most efficient way possible. It could almost be said that overcoming constraints is the main function of management. Some of the constraints are real and others are imaginary and certainly management in any organisation have to understand the constraints they have to work under. It is only when the nature of constraints is understood that action can be devised to modify them in a way that will increase efficiency.

Real constraints are inescapable and have to be dealt with in the most efficient way possible. Many of the real constraints have their origins in legislation. An illustrative sample of real constraints in a commercial organisation is given in Table 5.1. The imaginary constraints are in many ways the most difficult to deal with or eliminate. Table 5.2 gives an illustrative sample of imaginary constraints that are character-istic of a commercial type of organisation. I stress that Tables 5.1 and 5.2 only give a sample of the constraints that have to be considered. A rather more dramatic illustration of the relation between constraints is given in Figure 5.1 which shows the constraints as sets interacting with the management function. In reality the nature of the interaction depends on the aims and function of the management involved. It is also stressed that in many ways the actions of constraints have a certain amount of uncertainty associated with them. This uncertainty has to be allowed for in the assessment of options and in decision making.

Compared with a commercial organisation a civil service type of organisation will have a different perception of the set of imaginary constraints it has to deal with. A sample of the civil service type of imaginary constraints is given in Table 5.3. It should be noticed that the constraints are very much of the uncertainty about the future type, and that with the passage of time the significance and impact of such constraints/uncertainties will be resolved.

TABLE 5.1   An illustrative sample of real management constraints in a commercial organisation

Constraints	Implications
Tax level	The level of tax limits the funds available for developing the company
Regulations about working hours	Has a direct impact on the wage bill
Health and safety legislation	Requires companies to spend a certain amount of money to satisfy the regulations
Planning legislation	Puts limits on where offices and factories can be built
State of economy	Change in demand
Competition	Changes in demand for company's product
Bad debts	Customers default on repaying loans or paying for goods; this damages profits

TABLE 5.2   An illustrative sample of imaginary management constraints in a commercial organisation

Constraints	Implications
Staff cannot be retrained	Staff cannot adapt to changing circumstances
Profit margins cannot be changed	Price must always include the same profit margin regardless of consequences for market share
New products cannot be introduced	No allowance for changes in the pattern of product demanded
Decisions must always be approved by senior authority	Manager and team feel excluded from real decision making; also, the management hierarchy tends to become longer
Additional funds not available	No funds available for expansion or more modern equipment. Need to identify other forms of finance

In the following the two types of constraint are first considered separately. Real constraints are considered first and then imaginary constraints. Finally some general conclusions are drawn about constraints and their implications.

FIGURE 5.1   Real and imaginary constraints on management action

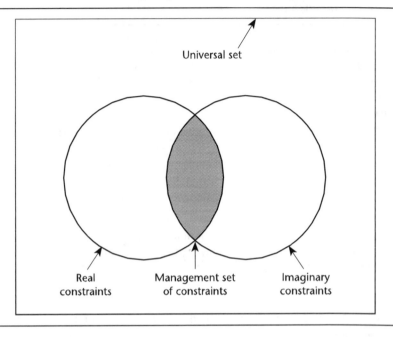

Real constraints

Real constraints have two main origins, one origin is legislation and the other is the conventions built up by the people in the enterprise itself. Legislation, although it may be difficult to interpret, is normally stated positively. The complete portfolio of constraints inherent in an enterprise is more difficult to identify and deal with as they may be enveloped in long-established rigid conventions in the way work is done. This envelopment of real constraints in conventions sometimes makes them hard to distinguish from imaginary constraints.

The real legal constraints range from working time legislation (Statutory Instrument 1998) and health and safety legislation to tax and insolvency legislation.

Legal constraints

To explain the nature of constraints, the legal constraints associated with hours of work are considered. In most European countries hours of work are constrained. For example, under European legislation an employer

TABLE 5.3 An illlustrative sample of imaginary constraints in a civil service type of organisation

Constraint	Implication
Need to take account of political acceptability	Party politics, and party election manifestos have to be taken into account. Also around election time it may be difficult to get decisions made.
Action constrained by existing legislation	Action to change way of working may require a change in legislation and this may take a considerable amount of time to change.
Budget cuts maybe imposed by the Treasury	A particular service may still have to be provided despite having to operate on a reduced budget. This may lead to reductions in staff causing delays in operations and an overall loss of efficiency.
Difficult to reduce staff levels	Ways have to be found to reduce staff to take account of more efficient ways of working.
Service provided cannot be changed	The process of changing service provided has to be initiated.

must not assign an adult worker as a night worker, or a young worker to work between 10pm and 6am, unless the worker has a health assessment before taking up the assignment, or had an assessment before being assigned on an earlier occasion and the employer has no reason to believe the assessment is no longer valid. The worker must also have an opportunity for a free health check at regular intervals. The assessment of young workers must also include identifying their capability to undertake the work. The young worker requirements do not apply to work defined as being 'of exceptional nature'; an 'exceptional nature' is understood as work of an emergency nature.

Where night workers are suffering from health problems recognised as being connected with night work, they should, wherever possible, be transferred to work to which they are suited and which is carried out during periods that would mean they cease to be a night worker.

Rest breaks and rest periods are also controlled by regulations. Under the regulations, an adult is entitled to a daily rest period of 11 consecutive hours per 24-hour period; and young workers are entitled to 12 hours (the rest period for young workers may be interrupted for activities involving periods of work that are short or split up over the day).

An adult is entitled to an uninterrupted weekly rest period of 24 hours in each seven-day period. The regulations allow an employer the flexibility to decide that the rest period can be taken as a 48-hour break in each 14-day period. The period must not include the daily rest period, unless justified by 'objective, technical or work organisation conditions'. Young workers are entitled to two days, consecutive if possible, in each seven-day period. This may be interrupted where activities are split up or are of short duration, and may be reduced where justified by technical or organisational reasons to not less than 36 consecutive hours.

Employees are also entitled to a daily rest break when the working day exceeds six hours. The duration and terms of the break should be determined by collective or workshop agreement. The break should be not less than 20 minutes, and can be spent away from the workstation.

There is an important set of exemptions to these regulations and they include:

1 air, rail, road, sea, inland waterway and lake transport;

2 sea fishing;

3 other work at sea;

4 the activities of doctors in training;

5 certain specified services such as the armed forces or the police, or certain specific activities in the civil protection services;

6 a worker employed as a domestic servant in a private household;

7 a worker where, on account of the specific characteristics of the activity in which he/she is engaged, the duration of his/her working time is not measured or predetermined or can be determined by the worker. These people include: managing executives or other persons with autonomous decision-taking powers; family workers; workers officiating at religious ceremonies in churches and religious communities;

8 a worker whose activities are such that his/her place of work and place of residence are distant from one another or his/her different places of work are distant from one another;

9 workers engaged in security and surveillance activities requiring a permanent presence in order to protect property or persons, as may be the case for security guards and caretakers or security firms;

10   workers involved in activities that need continuity of service or production, as may be the case in relation to:

> services relating to the reception, treatment or care of people in hospitals or similar establishments, residential institutions and prisons;

> work at docks or airports;

> press, radio, television, cinematographic production, postal and telecommunications services and civil protection services;

> gas, water and electricity production, transmission and distribution, household refuse collection and incineration;

> industries in which work cannot be interrupted on technical grounds;

> research and development activities;

> agriculture;

11   where there are foreseeable surges of activity, as may be the case in: agriculture, tourism and postal services;

12   also workers are exempt from the regulations when unusual and unexpected events occur that are beyond the control of the worker's employer, or when there is an accident or the imminent risk of an accident.

Also all employers have to satisfy the government's equal opportunity policy as defined in the Sex Discrimination Act 1975, The Race Relations Act 1976 and The Disabled Person and Employment Act 1944. This policy can involve the employer in extra costs for training and for the provision of special equipment and facilities for disabled people. It may also be that work schedules have to be adjusted to accommodate disabled people's capacity.

Another very real set of constraints are those imposed by health and safety legislation:

The health and safety arrangements most organisations have to satisfy are national regulations so it is important to understand the nature of their background. It is also important to recognise that there are also important international regulations that have to be satisfied. International regulations include European Union directives.

The development of legislation to improve the health and safety of working conditions in British industry has a long history. The first legislation to improve working conditions was the Health and Morals of Apprentices Act of 1802. The principle of government inspection of factories was introduced by the Factory Act of 1833, around the time that slavery was abolished. Although health and safety legislation has been iteratively refined over the years a watershed in the development in legislation came in 1970 when Mrs Barbara Castle appointed the Robens Committee to make a review of all safety legislation to determine its relevance to the needs of the late twentieth century. The findings of the committee ultimately led to the Health and Safety at Work Act of 1974 being passed and the introduction of quite dramatic changes in the way health and safety matters are handled.

Since the Health and Safety at Work Act was passed there have been many changes to the range of responsibilities of the Health and Safety Executive and the regulations in force. Before the Health and Safety at Work Act was put into operation responsibility for many safety issues was divided between various departments, for example: responsibility for the safety of offshore oil and gas installations lay with the Department of Energy; responsibility for railway safety lay with the Department of Transport; and responsibility for the safety of nuclear installations owned by UKAEA lay with the UKAEA. Over the years these responsibilities have been unified under the aegis of the Health and Safety Executive.

Two important influences act upon the Health and Safety Executive to develop regulations: European Union legislation and major accidents. Sometimes these influences combine to intensify pressure for change and additional regulation. Examples of this process are:

(1) A series of serious chemical plant accidents around Europe led to the European Commission issuing a Directive on Major Hazards, in 1982, which led to the Health and Safety Executive forming the Major Hazards Assessment Unit. (2) The accident on the Piper Alpha Oil Rig in 1988 led to responsibility for the safety of offshore oil and gas installations being moved from the Department of Energy to the Health and Safety Executive and to the Health and Safety Executive issuing the Offshore Installation Safety Regulations. (3) Concern about the fatal accident rate in the construction industry being five times higher than the average for all industry led to the introduction of the Construction (Design and Management) Regulations 1994.

Apart from the Construction (Design and Management) Regulations 1994, the most important group of recent regulations is known as the Six Pack. The Six Pack regulations were issued in response to a series of European Union directives and cover: Management of Health and Safety at Work, Workplace (Health, Safety and Welfare), Provision and Use of

Work Equipment Regulations, Personal Protective Equipment at Work, Health and Safety (Display Screen Equipment), and Manual Handling.

The Management of Health and Safety at Work Regulations 1992 introduced the requirement for every employer to have an assessment made of all the risks their employees are exposed to and to provide employees with such health surveillance as is appropriate to the risk they are exposed to in their work. An employer also has to confirm that employees are competent to undertake the work they have to do.

Local government action is constrained by the Local Government Acts 1988 and 1997 (*Local Government Act* 1988 and 1992). The many sections of the Act are formal legal constraints on the way local government organisations can act. Among the many constraints it includes is specification of the way local government organisations should deal with the supply of goods or materials and the execution of work. Section 135 of the Act is important in encouraging competition as it requires that contracting processes shall include provisions for securing competition among suppliers.

Financial constraints are also very real, these involve: accounting practices, borrowing limits and direct and indirect taxation. It is not intended to deal with taxation constraints in fine detail, but simply to draw attention to their importance to managers. Sometimes financial constraints are introduced almost by accident. A company accepting a loan or grant from the government may have to accept special constraints as a condition of accepting the funding.

Company legislation includes the Companies Act 1985 and the Insolvency Act 1986 and this legislation imposes personal liability on directors of companies found guilty of offences or non-compliance. There are also duties imposed on particular types of companies and businesses by various regulatory authorities such as The Stock Exchange, the Take-Over Panel and other self-regulatory organisations. All employees from trainees through to managing directors have a responsibility to ensure that people who may be affected by their actions do not suffer as a result of a mistake or failure to carry out a particular task properly.

The fact that the directors of a company are the joint custodians of the company's business and assets means that the board can only function properly where mutual trust exists. Although individual directors sometimes begrudge the need to return to the board for authority to take certain actions, the board regime can provide a discipline and protection which significantly limits the inherent risks for each individual board member. This brings out a beneficial aspect that may be associated with some constraints and the need for clear precise communication between all parties involved in managing an activity.

In any communication there are important constraints. Communication must be efficient and there are upper and lower limits to efficient communication. There are those that mistakenly consider that efficient communication depends on delaying everybody in the organisation with long gossipy telephone calls, faxes and e-mails. At the other extreme there are those that believe no communication is the most efficient way of participating in the life of an organisation. Efficient communication is a balance between the two extremes.

Imaginary constraints

Many imaginary constraints have their origins in the people directly involved in the organisation. The decision makers involved in the organisation may have a blinkered view of the future and the way the market and organisation may be developed. These people may be too comfortable and satisfied with the status quo or they may just be too phlegmatic to push for improvements. This blinkered view can happen in both private and government organisations. In a government organisation imaginary constraints may be reinforced by the fact that any change to the way the organisation operates may need a change in legislation.

It is not possible to be certain about what causes the growth in the resistance to change. Attention is drawn to the difficulty in correlating acceptability of risk with cultural characteristics of the population involved. Acceptability of risk could be equated with imaginary constraints. The work of Brenot, Bonnefous and Marris shows something of the depth of uncertainty in correlating acceptability of risk with cultural factors (Brenot *et al.* 1998). Aversion to risk is very similar to resistance to change and is a form of imaginary constraint.

Another way of classifying imaginary constraints is to consider them as those that are internal to an organisation and those that are external to an organisation.

The internal imaginary constraints are those likely to be associated with the decision makers in the organisation of interest. These are most likely only to change if the ownership or control of the organisation changes, although it is possible that some changes may be brought about by training or the injection of more flexible staff.

External imaginary constraints are likely to be more difficult to change and even more difficult to say how and when they will change. External constraints may vary in an almost emotional way. The changes could be considered as unpredictable as voting in a parliamentary election or the changes in a market. No government stays in power for ever but it is very difficult to predict when they will change. Markets are always changing; for example, new foods, new computers, new models of cars are often being introduced. It is the nature of external imaginary constraints that they assume, without any evidence, that in the future the operational environment external to the organisation will be different to that which can reasonably be predicted. This means that imaginary external constraints may, in some cases, turn out to be a better prediction of future reality than a prediction based on current trends.

Imaginary constraints are by their nature often very difficult barriers for a manager to deal with. Such constraints often have a permanence similar to the permanence of myths and legends. In a similar way imaginary constraints are often the product of misunderstandings due to poor communications. The fact that imaginary constraints develop shows weaknesses in the management system. Like myths, imaginary constraints often develop from some small, often invented fact which is continuously embroidered until it is believed to be part of the real world. In Table 5.4 some imaginary constraints, their possible origin and action needed to deal with them are identified.

It is important to remember that it takes time for imaginary constraints to develop, and it takes time to deal with them. Imaginary constraints cannot be eliminated instantly. Even with superb communications it takes time for vital information about new views on ways of dealing with and managing constraints to filter through an organisation and be acted upon.

At an election politicians may make brave speeches about the legislation they are going to introduce if they are elected. Not all the promises will be kept and if legislation is introduced it will often only become effective several years after its first mention. This makes it very difficult for decision makers to allow for such changes in advance.

The decision makers in any organisation have to be blessed with a certain amount of political acumen to judge the impact of new legislation and when it will have an impact on an organisation's operations.

Similar arguments can be made about any real constraints such as changes in the market or the development of new products.

Conclusions

Managers and entrepreneurs have to recognise the nature and importance of the constraints on their actions. Some constraints like those based on

TABLE 5.4 Some imaginary constraints, their possible origin and action needed to deal with them

Constraint	Possible origins	Action needed to deal with them
Design cannot be changed	Design team does not want to take on more work or there is friction between units in an organisation	Action needed to reorganise the design team so that it can willingly undertake the work
Production cannot be increased	There have been some problems in achieving present level of production	A detailed study needed to determine the real limits to production
New insurance products cannot be introduced	People unused to the concept of new insurance products	Test marketing to determine acceptability of new product and training needed on how to sell new products
Workforce not in touch with new technology	No attempt has been made to train workforce in new technology	Introduce an appropriate training programme
Difficult to recruit new staff	At past salary levels it has been difficult to recruit staff	Sound out the market with a sample test and revise salary scales
Union opposed to new development	Proposal has not been properly explained to the union	Proposal carefully explained to the union
Funding for new developments not available	In the past no deviation from budget allowed or alternative funding allowed	New ways of obtaining funds to be found and explained

legislation are real. Other constraints are imaginary and have the characteristics of myths and legends. Such imaginary constraints often have their origins in poor communications.

Constraints are present in every phase of an organisation's activity and in order to improve efficiency it is generally necessary to eliminate or at least modify them or find a better way of living with them. It is appreciated that where it is wished to modify constraints based on legislation it might take a very long time and a lot of effort to achieve the required modification.

Important constraints that have to be considered are summarised in Table 5.5.

TABLE 5.5 Summary of real and imaginary constraints

Real constraints	Imaginary constraints
Tax level	Staff cannot be retrained
State of national economy	Profit margins cannot be changed
Commercial legislation	New products cannot be introduced
Bad debts	Extra funding cannot be raised
Competition	Management structure cannot be simplified
Working hours regulation	Staff numbers cannot be reduced
Health and safety legislation	Political pressures have to be solved
Race Relations Act Sex Discrimination Act	} Will reduce the efficiency of the organisation
European Commission Directive	Cannot be adapted to local conditions and needs

Constraints play an important part in determining the magnitude of uncertainty associated with any proposed enterprise.

References

Brenot, J., Bonnefous, S. Marris, C. (1998) 'Testing the cultural theory of risk in France', *Risk Analysis* 18(6), December: 729–39.

Local Government Act (1988) London: Her Majesty's Stationery Office.

Local Government Act (1992) London: Her Majesty's Stationery Office.

Statutory Instrument (1998) *The Working Time Regulations 1998*, no. 1833, London: Her Majesty's Stationery Office.

CHAPTER SIX

The reality of management in local government

As shown by the cases considered in Chapter 4, there is considerable similarity between a central government organisation and a local government organisation. Two very important differences are:

1 Local government organisations by the very nature of their role work closer to the public and the elected members.

2 Many local government functions and financial resources are dictated by central government.

Typically a county council may have responsibility for: education, fire and rescue services, police, county property, libraries, planning, county environmental issues, probation service, social services, trading standards and transportation including roads and bridges. Some counties have extensive property including: houses, farms, schools and country parks. District/borough councils are by definition much smaller than county councils, on average about a tenth of the size of a county council. Funding for some of their activities is in the form of a grant direct from the county council. Typically a district/borough council's responsibilities includes: planning, sewers and drainage, housing, environmental health, listed buildings, pest control, refuse collection, council tax, building controls, electoral role and council tax (*Hertfordshire The Official Guide* 1997).

The basic control of central government over local government activities is via the budget. The size of the budget is constrained by central government treasury directives. Allocation of funds within budget constraints is determined partly by legal obligations, the council on the advice of its staff and partly pressure applied by elected members. Each year as the budget is being prepared there is great debate and bargaining between local government units about what their share of the budget will be. If a unit's share is reduced cuts have to be made either in services provided or in staff. Conversely if their share of the budget is increased services and staff may be increased.

The process by which local government bodies allocate the funds that they are authorised to allocate is a major influence on the form of the management process. Winning or defending a budget allocation is a vital management activity, as without funds there can be no activity. This leads to the central management question of how to allocate priority to the various candidates for funding.

In recent years, as a matter of government policy aimed at improving efficiency, many local government services have been privatised or outsourced. Privatisation was given a considerable boost by Norman Lamont in 1992 when, as Chancellor, he introduced the Private Finance Initiative (Smith 1999). Often all that has happened is that county council units have been taken over by a private company and the county council has to buy back the service from the private companies involved. The cost of the private company doing the job is supposed to be lower than the cost of the council doing it with its own staff. The reasons given for the assumption of lower costs when work is done by private industry are claimed to be that: (1) private industry is more efficient than a local government organisation, (2) private industry is more flexible. This could be taken as a rather sad commentary on the efficiency of local government organisations, but it is a very difficult case to prove either way. The privatisation of local government functions has one potentially damaging implication for local government, which is that in many cases it reduces or even eliminates local government's ability to deal with some complex technical issues themselves, the reason being that the professional staff with appropriate technical skills have all been moved to the private company that has taken over the work and staff. This means that if a complex technical issue has to be assessed either an expensive specialist contractor or a consultant has to be called in. This situation is also likely to give rise to the formation of a committee to assess the evidence and advise on the action to be taken. The committee process delays action being taken, a situation which is likely to generate further problems. This problem is discussed further in the next chapter.

So what can be done to improve the efficiency of local government management? The problem has to be tackled at three levels: (1) redefining the basic role of local government, (2) improving the efficiency of individual managers, (3) providing managers with better tools.

Redefining the role of local government

Possibly any major improvement in management efficiency can only be achieved by refining the role of local government. It is accepted that major changes in the structure of local government will require changes in legislation which have to be approved by parliament and will by their very nature take a long time to bring about. Without changing the structure of local government it is often supposed that no real improvement in management efficiency can be brought about. However, I believe it is useful to explore the other options to expose ways efficiency can be improved. Some of the weaknesses of local government are in many ways due to the fact that local government has over time grown in a haphazard way. A realistic analysis of the situation must start by questioning the aims, nature and justification of local government. In Table 6.1 the ideal aims of local government are identified. It is stressed that they are the ideal aims and not those set by legislation. The difference between ideal and actual aims helps to identify where it may be possible to improve efficiency.

In Table 6.2 an attempt is made to identify the differences between ideal and real aims. The general causes of the differences between ideal and real aims are restrictions on funding and legislation. Funding and legislation are at the root of most constraints on local government action. Without extra funding additional activities cannot be undertaken. It may be the extra funding required can be made available by savings resulting from improving the efficiency with which existing activities are performed.

Local government activities are complex and any attempt to improve efficiency requires a multi-disciplinary approach. It may be possible to improve the efficiency by rationalising the way some operations are performed. The question is what scope is there for such rationalisation in local government activities? Some possible ways of rationalising local government operations are suggested in Table 6.3. It is admitted that some of the ways proposed are quite radical and would require a major change in political thinking.

There are usually advantages and disadvantages in making changes to the way local government is managed. In the following I give what I hope is a balanced unbiased assessment of the advantages and disadvantages of the changes to the way local government operates implied in Table 6.3. If nothing else the assessment exposes some of the considerations any manager has to take into account in trying to improve an organisation.

TABLE 6.1   Identification of the ideal aims for local government

Aim	Action involved
Provide adequate high-quality education for all in the community	Provide and staff schools and colleges on a scale adjusted to current demographic patterns
Provide fire and rescue services for the community	Provide fire and rescue services appropriate to each community
Provide police/probation service	Provide a police/probationary service appropriate to each community
Provide trading standards service	Provide a trading standards service appropriate to each community
Provide social services	Provide social services appropriate to the community (the social services to be provided are at present laid down by central government legislation)
Provide a unified transport system	Develop a unified transport system to satisfy the needs of each community and improve the overall efficiency of transport for everyone
Provide a planning and environment service	Provide a planning and environment service that ensures, as far as practical, a pleasant environment for the whole community to live and work in
Provide a library service	Provide a library service appropriate to the needs of each community
Provide property required by the community	Provide or stimulate provision of property – houses and open spaces required by the community
Provide and maintain roads and bridges required	Ensure that existing roads and bridges for which it is responsible are properly maintained and that roads and bridges are built to satisfy transport needs in the foreseeable future

Limiting the time public inquiries are allowed to take can save costs directly both for the organisations applying for permission and for the organisations that grant or refuse the application. The process is often defended as being an essential democratic process, but in practice it is just a bureaucratic exercise. Currently the public affected by the decision are not allowed a direct vote on the acceptability of a proposal. The decisions are made behind closed doors. So to make the system democratic it would be necessary to break down the current mock democracy façade. This

TABLE 6.2 Differences between ideal and real aims

Ideal aim	Difference between ideal and real aims
Provide high-quality education for all children	Satisfaction of ideal aim limited and constrained by government spending policy
Provide comprehensive fire and rescue services	Comprehensive satisfaction limited by funding and the fact that not all emergency conditions can be predicted and some emergencies are so rare they are dealt with on an *ad hoc* basis
Provide police/probation service	Provision limited by funding, but needs can change quite rapidly and it should be possible to adjust resources equally quickly
Provide trading standards service	In the real case the scope of the service required is always changing as consumption patterns change; within funding controlling the service provided must be adjusted to match conditions
Provide social services	The service provided is determined by legislation, there is scope for improving the efficiency with which it is provided and by eliminating fraud
Provide unified transport service	Because of difference between communities it is difficult to define what is required in universally applicable terms
Provide planning and environment service	Service provided should reflect public demands and aspirations. Planners should show leadership by taking the long-term view of what is likely to be in the best interests of the community
Provide library service	Service provided should reflect public demand and interests
Provide property required	Property acquired and disposed of should match exactly current and predicted requirements. Government policy will dictate the portfolio of buildings required
Provide and maintain roads and bridges required	Maintenance and new construction limited by funding available, therefore done on a priority basis

would save time for everyone involved, make the system more transparent and improve the overall efficiency.

Putting the fire and rescue services under control of the insurance industry might seem like a retrograde step but it need not be so. It could

TABLE 6.3 Some possible ways of rationalising local government activity

Activity	Possible rationalisation
Time- and resource-consuming public inquiries into planning applications	Set a strict timetable for arriving at decisions and ensure the timetable is kept to. (This would be a saving for both private and public organisations)
Fire and rescue services	Have this funded by the insurance industry, as it once was
Raising required funds	Freedom from Treasury controls
Provision of social services	Divide this into two parts which are: (1) a benefit paying agency operated as a central government department; (2) a caring agency that would look after the old and infirm and those with disabilities
Reduce the number of councils	Reducing the number of councils would reduce the number and size of administrative units required
Put a positive limit on debating time	This would reduce discussion, keep debating time to a minimum and save time for all parties involved
Put a limit on the number of committees and their life	This would increase the time available for productive effort

be seen as a form of privatisation. The insurance industry wants to keep claims as low as possible so it has an incentive to deal with fires and other emergencies as fast and as efficiently as possible. The problems might be how to arrange for the insurance industry to be paid for providing the service and how to make sure the service provided satisfies the required standards. Funding could be partly paid for by a levy on premiums and insisting everyone has insurance. Another option would be for local government to pay the insurance industry to run the service. The quality of the service would be ensured by independent inspectors.

The funding of local government should be freed from central government control and local government allowed to raise money on the open market. This type of funding need not be just fixed interest stock; it could be some kind of dividend earning share which would encourage local government to operate on a profit earning basis. To adopt such an approval would require extensive rethinking about the way local government is financed and is paid for the services it provides. Such changes would have to be carefully policed to ensure that there was no element of fraud in the operation.

Provision of social services is one of the major costs of local government. The two main parts of the service are paying benefits and providing various services to help the disadvantaged. The benefit paying service could be regarded as a banking-type service, except that the customers do not directly have to put money in. It is possible to envisage the service being provided by a bank for a fee, again another form of privatisation. With any money handling activity the risk of fraud is high and certainly false benefit claims are not unknown. Providing services to the disadvantaged and disabled is a difficult problem and does require sympathetic attention. There may be some benefit in making provision of social care the responsibility of a unified self-contained body centrally funded and centrally provided.

Four of the seven suggestions postulated in Table 6.3 seem more likely than the others to improve the efficiency of local government, and they are also more radical than the others. To implement them would require significant changes in legislation. The four suggestions are: freedom to raise funds, reduce the number of councils, limit debating time and limit the number of committees allowed.

The justification for giving freedom to councils in the way they raise the funds they require is that it would give them greater freedom in deciding the range of activities they undertake and the timing of the projects they undertake. There is also a possible negative side to giving councils freedom to raise whatever funds they require. The negative side is that if they raise a lot of money in the open market they could disturb the national economy, so some form of control would still be required. Also it is possible that it could lead to gross inconsistency in the services that councils provide.

The motives for reducing the number of councils are that there is an optimum size for most organisations and there is an overlap in the activities of district councils and county councils. This overlap almost amounts to duplication of effort. To prevent councils developing in widely different ways there would have to be a legally binding specification defining the consistent way in which councils must discharge their responsibilities, this specification being designed so that councils satisfy as far as possible the aims mentioned earlier. The change would mean that instead of having several levels of local government there would be just one level. In other words the local government system would be thinned down. It would also mean that anyone wanting to stimulate local government into action would have only one level of organisation to deal with. This does not mean that the change would instantly be successful, it would need considerable care and attention to make it work, but in the long term it should speed decision making and there would not be so many ways decisions could be delayed.

One activity that takes a lot of time in local government, as in central government, is the time the elected politicians take in debating a proposal. One problem is that the elected members do not have detailed understanding of all the technical, economic and socio-political implications of the issue being debated. They often concentrate on petty political point scoring using evidence that has been spin doctored away from precise information. The detrimental effect of such practices would be reduced if debating time was limited and all contributions had to be accurate and specifically related to the issue being debated. This also means that officials would have to be even more careful in preparing proposals and briefs, making them as precise and objective as possible.

Another activity that takes a lot of time in both local and national government organisations is committee work. Dependence on committees is often a sign that the organisation involved does not have adequate knowledge to assess the issues and reach logical decisions.

The two main reasons for committees being formed are:

1   to advise management

2   to approve the acceptability of proposals put before them.

The first justification for a committee, that of advising management, is in some ways easy to justify. Management may not have the skills or knowledge to deal with a particular problem and therefore has to seek advice from specialists in the field. Rules for selecting experts are set out in Chicken (1996) and a slight rewording of the rules to make them appropriate to local government decision making is as follows:

1   Experts consulted should have expertise in the field in which their opinion is being sought.

2   Experts should be asked to identify evidence that tends to contradict their views as well as evidence that supports their views.

3   The size of the problem on which expert opinion is sought should be kept to an understandable level. In other words the problem or problems should be decomposed to a size for which it is realistic to find a solution.

4   Analysis of the views of several experts is better than the view of a single expert.

5   Opinions must be sought in a structured way as unstructured questioning can produce misleading results.

6   Statistical analysis of the opinions expressed is better than a subjective view. Provided the questions are structured and even if opinions expressed are subjective statistical analysis helps identification and assessment of the associated uncertainty.

If a committee is formed for the purpose of discussing possible solutions to a problem it should be disbanded as soon as the discussion is complete. In a paper by the UK government's Office of Science and Technology that examined the use of scientific advice in policy making, among the many points the paper made three are relevant to any management policy making situation such as managers in local government may be involved in (*The Use of Scientific Advice in Policy Making* 1997: 4, 6–7). The points slightly rephrased are:

1   Openness in presenting and explaining advice will help promote informed discussion and assessment of any proposition made that is based on the advice.

2   Problems may arise with little or no warning and management should have plans ready to enable them to react quickly to get the appropriate advice on how to deal with the issue.

3   When the conclusions presented by advisers expose greater uncertainties or conflicting opinions there will be considerable difficulty in resolving the issue.

To be able to reduce the number of committees does mean that there have to be advisers available who have the required knowledge of the propositions being considered and the ability to assess them and reach sound decisions about the action required. The advisers may be permanent officials or known specialists who can be called on as the need arises. It is appreciated that specialist advisers may need appropriate support staff, but specialist advisers are likely to reach decisions faster than committees.

Improving the efficiency of individual managers

What has just been said about refining the basic role of local government has a direct bearing on the potential ways the efficiency of individual managers can be improved. As more services of local government are privatised the function and operation of local government changes. Although functions are privatised it does not necessarily mean that local government loses all responsibility for the activity. The precise delegation of responsibility will in each case depend on the particular privatisation contract and the nature of the activity. In every case the local government will have some responsibility for the privatised activity, not merely because it has to pay for the service that is provided by the privatised organisation. What in some ways is more important is that local government has to have the resources to check that what it orders and what it receives from private industry is what it wants. This requires well-skilled resources.

For example if maintenance of roads and street lighting is privatised, the local government organisation, in whose area the work falls, will still have to specify what should be done and check that the work is done to specification. Similarly if a local government organisation has privatised its bill and salary paying function, it will have to check that the paying organisation knows what to pay and to whom. Also it will have to check that the payments are made correctly.

The reorganisation of local government functions resulting from the privatisation of various local government activities means that the managers left on the local government payroll have a rather different and in some ways more difficult job. The new or different problems they have to deal with are:

1   All work required has to be specified to the privatised organisation.

2   The price for the work has to be agreed with the privatised organisation.

3   A check has to be made that the privatised organisation has done the work correctly.

Given that managers have to operate in a different way they must be trained in how to deal effectively and efficiently with the new situation. Five vital components of this training are:

1   Understanding of the contractual obligations of dealing with privatised industry. For example, how well is the client protected against any claims the privatised industry may make against it?

2   Are there any residual health and safety responsibilities that the privatised industry shares with the client? To deal with these factors needs a wide understanding of health and safety legislation.

3   How to check that what the privatised industry contracted to do has been done in the way the client wanted it done.

4   How to establish the order of priority for each task in the portfolio of tasks requiring attention.

5   Understanding the political process and its impact on the work of local government.

Training in the five components is not an alternative to normal professional training whether it is engineering, architecture, accountancy, planning, transport or environment but it is an essential supplement to normal professional training.

Providing managers with better tools

This problem is more about adequate communication and data than it is about computers. It is assumed that any modern major organisation is well equipped with an appropriate computer system. At the same time it is recognised that the computers may not be used as aids as effectively as they could be.

Units in a local authority may be euphemistically called 'cost centres' or 'business units'; this suggests an element of entrepreneurism, which is not altogether misplaced. Given the regime of the annual budget each cost centre/business unit has to operate in a commercial way to ensure that its expenditure is kept within budget. There is no bonus or commission in local government for keeping within budget – such incentives are confined to private industry. Local government is, as already mentioned, constrained by legislation in what it can do and constrained by the Treasury in what it can spend. Around the world there are many variations of this approach.

One interesting case is what happened in Friedrichshafen in Germany when Count Von Zeppelin died. He left the vast majority of his shares in his companies that were based in Friedrichshafen to the town of Friedrichshafen. Count Von Zeppelin's firms are very prosperous so the town has a handsome income from the shares it inherited. This has allowed the town to spend money on a multi-purpose concert hall and other amenities. Another twist to this story is that the Burgomaster of Friedrichshafen also has to serve as Chairman of Count Von Zeppelin's companies, which are still major employers in the area.

At the heart of providing managers with better tools is providing them with more flexibility in the way they raise and use the money allocated to them by the budget.

If managers were allowed greater flexibility in using the funds allocated to them in the budget and also allowed to raise money on the financial market for projects, they would be able to operate in a more dynamic way. This assumes that any project they proposed funding in this way would yield a return on the money invested that would be adequate to pay the interest on and repay the money borrowed.

Ideally the process of making money available should be as quick as it is in private industry and long delays due to the views of a multitude of committees having to be sought would be avoided. If those conditions were achieved the chief executive of a county council or district council would be able to operate in a more dynamic way, responding to demands quicker. In addition, better financial control would give managers of proposed developments a better organisational structure, and perhaps even reduce the levels in their management hierarchy.

Conclusions

There are several ways local government efficiency can be improved. The rationalisation required to bring about these improvements demands simplification of the structure of local government. It also requires both elected and official members of the organisation should have a very detailed knowledge and understanding of the technical, economic and socio-political aspects of the issues to be dealt with. They should also have the capability of assessing the evidence and arriving at sound and defensible decisions without involving rooms full of committees that only partly understand the issues involved.

To make the system more dynamic it is proposed financial control should be simplified and managers allowed the freedom to raise finance for the projects they could justify on the basis that they would earn an adequate return on the money invested and not be a burden on the taxpayer.

References

Chicken, J.C. (1996) *Risk Handbook*, London: International Business Press, p. 264–265.

Hertfordshire The Official Guide (1997) Cheltenham: Centurion for Hertford-shire County Council.

Smith. A.J. (1999) *Privatised Infrastructure: The Role of Government*, London: Thomas Telford, p. 221.

The Use of Scientific Advice in Policy Making (1997), London: Department of Trade and Industry for the Office of Science and Technology, pp. 4, 6–7.

CHAPTER SEVEN

The reality of management in central government

To put the problem of managing the civil service into perspective it helps to understand the size of the organisation and the diversity of its activities. In 1997 it had a staff of 475 339, down from 565 319 in 1992 (*Civil Service Yearbook* 1998: XCViii). Of the 58 departments the five largest were: Defence 109 206 employees, Social Security 93 055 employees, the Inland Revenue 54 029 employees, HM Prison Service 37 704 employees and Education and Employment 33 662 (ibid.). One interesting, but in my view optimistic, government view to which the editorial of the 1998 *Civil Service Yearbook* drew attention was that by the year 2002 one quarter of the dealings the government has with the public will be done electronically.

As shown by the cases examined in Chapter 4, in many ways management in central government organisations could be regarded as management in a strait-jacket. The constraints on management in central government organisations are different to local government constraints and different to those that exist in private industry. The major constraints are:

1   A great body of past legislation.

2   A very large committee structure (including parliament itself).

3   Funding available set by the Treasury.

4   The need to be responsive to the political situation and the views of elected members.

These constraints show why central government organisations are structured in a different way to local government and private industry organisations. There are very broadly two main functions of central government organisations, which could almost be regarded as two levels of operation. The functions are:

1   Advising government.

2   Providing some service defined by legislation.

These functions could be regarded as defining the two main levels in the hierarchy of civil service type organisations. The basic structure of a typical central government department is shown in Figure 7.1. It is stressed that the structure shown is for a hypothetical department and is just intended to show the general characteristics rather than the specific characteristics of a particular department. The units shown will not exist in isolation but will interact with other government and public bodies.

The responsibilities of the head of department will include: (1) advising ministers on matters relevant to the department's function, (2) ensuring that the department operates efficiently and fulfils the role set for it, (3) as far as possible operates within the allowed budget. Major constraints on the operation and management of a typical department are summarised in Table 7.1 and an indication given of the implications

FIGURE 7.1   The basic structure of a typical central government department

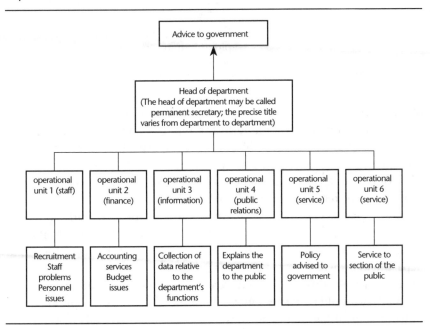

Note: The size of blocks describing the units does not imply the number of employees or their importance.

TABLE 7.1 Constraints on the operation and management of a typical central government department

Constraint	Implications
Defining legislation	Sets out limits to action that can be taken and what has to be done
Funding	Funding available might be set in broad terms by legislation but to satisfy Treasury budget requirements cuts may be made. The cuts may reduce the capability of the department to fulfil its obligations under legislation
Staff	Competence of staff may be limited and numbers may mean only routine tasks can be dealt with. This means non-routine tasks are not dealt with
International commitments and agreements	International agreements may impose requirements on the way particular government functions are performed, e.g. how big should be the contribution to the forces' international units
Political environment	Attention always has to be given to the possibility that the politicians in power may introduce changes to the role for the department
A national emergency	Some disaster such as war, flood or epidemic may dramatically change the way the department is expected to operate

of the constraints. The list of constraints given is not comprehensive and is only intended as a guide to the types of constraint that have to be considered. In specific cases other constraints may be more important.

How the department is set up to provide the service it is expected to provide can be regarded as the seed from which the cancer of a committee structure grows. Generally departments are established with staff just sufficient in numbers and skills to perform the duties allocated to it. This means any unusual situation requiring skills not possessed by the department's own staff requires specialist staff or advisers to be called in. Then a committee is formed to assess the specialist's advice and the action that should be taken. Once a committee is formed people are often unwilling to disband it. The most likely action to be taken is for the committee to be given new or amended terms of reference. How the committee structure of a department grows is shown in a simplified

FIGURE 7.2 Growth of a department's committee structure

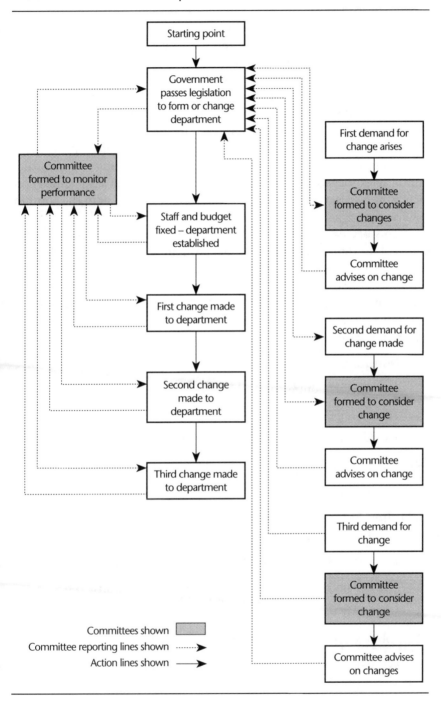

diagrammatic way in Figure 7.2. The figure shows how committees may proliferate as a result of each change in demand, with each change resulting in a new committee. In the case shown in Figure 7.2 it is possible to envisage that the committees formed to consider change would all have to report through the committees formed to monitor performance. It is possible that unless positive action is taken to close a committee down it will just continue to exist forever. There may even be a struggle to develop an order of seniority between the committees, with the findings of the newest or most junior committee having to be approved by the oldest or most senior committee before the findings can be implemented. The committee structure becomes a self-perpetuating way of life. Committees may grow like plants, with committees in an organisation increasing like leaves on a tree. But committees do not fall in the autumn like leaves.

This begins to expose a starting point for improving the management of a central government department as being improving its operational structure.

It is not suggested that no action has been taken to improve the management of the civil service, in fact there is a long history of reports recommending the changes that should be made. Important in these reports are (Jenkins *et al.* 1988: 3):

1   Northcote – Trevelyan Report of 1854

2   The Playfair Commission 1874–75

3   The Ridley Commission 1886–90

4   The MacDonnell Commission 1912–15

5   The Tomlin Commission 1929–31

6   The Fulton Report 1968

The Fulton Report noted six reasons which had contributed to the Civil Service not keeping up with its changing role; they were (ibid.):

1   The service was based on the philosophy of the amateur

2   The division into classes made for a cumbersome structure

3   Specialists had no authority

4   Too few civil servants were skilled managers

5   Whitehall had too little contact with the outside world

6   There were deficiencies in personnel management

Although the comments were specific to the time they referred to, they represent a useful check list for assessing the efficacy of any management structure either inside the civil service or in private industry.

The more recent report on the efficiency of the civil service (ibid.) followed very much the same theme as the Fulton Report. It drew attention to the difficulty of managing as a single entity an organisation with very diverse responsibilities and about half a million employees (ibid.: 4). The report also expressed considerable concern that senior management in the civil service was dominated by people whose skills are in policy formulation and have little experience of working where services are actually delivered (ibid.: 3).

The report also drew attention to the fact that due to increasing demands on ministers' time from parliament, the media and the public, ministers tended to be overloaded (ibid.: 4). This means they have not the time to devote to improving the efficiency of the civil service – a situation that can arise in a similar way in any large organisation. The authors of the report say yes to the view that to overcome the problem the structure of the civil service should be changed, the main change being that there should be a central civil service responsible for servicing ministers and managing departments (ibid.: 4). Supporting the departments should be agencies, with their own staff, responsible for providing the service the department is authorised to provide. To ensure that the necessary changes are properly planned and effectively implemented it was proposed that a very senior civil servant should be appointed the project manager with responsibility for making the necessary changes (ibid.). The project manager would report directly to the Prime Minster. This exposes the complexity of the management system in the civil service.

It is not suggested that one report instantly solves all the problems; because of the nature of the organisation, the pace of change is slow. Without a revolution change is likely to remain pedestrian. It may be because the pace of change is slow the problems grow faster than they are solved.

A major function of a central government organisation is to administer regulations. There has been concern that there are too many regulations and that they are an unnecessary burden on business. In an attempt to ensure that action is taken to minimise the impact of regulation the government established a Deregulation Task Force. In the government response to the Task Force's report for 1996, they mention that in the previous three years 750 regulations had been repealed or amended (ibid.: 13–16). Another report suggests that in 1979 there were 116 fewer statutes giving the right of entry and search (*The Government Response to the Deregulation Task Force Report 1996* 1997). For business premises alone there are 267 statutes giving inspectors the right to enter. There were 24 026 staff associated with inspecting businesses and in 1998 they made 466 000 inspections (ibid.: 'An inspector calls . . . and another' 1999: 31; Lake 1999: 24). In addition to inspections by national inspectors there are inspections by European Union inspectors. Now looking at the possible forms of central government management starting with the forms mentioned in Table 7.2, it is easy to understand how many of the possible forms of organisation have very significant political implications attached to them. To reduce staff or just employ people on short-term contracts would need to be approved by the government involved and to be supported by the trade unions. Working time would also have to comply with the relevant legislation.

The use of contractors might give rise to difficulties where sensitive or confidential information has to be handled. Also any form of short-term employment could make it difficult to deal with long-term projects efficiently. Another problem with short-term employment is that it is difficult to get the full commitment of such staff as they are likely to want to see some long-term career prospects.

In general there is no direct entrepreneurial aspect to the organisa-tion of a central government department. However, the work of a central government department may significantly influence the scope of the entrepreneur in the private sector. This influence may come through the government process of dealing with tenders for contracts for research, and contracts for the supply of goods and services. Slightly more indirect, but very important, influences on entrepreneurs are a government's: economic policy, changes in taxes, changes in the pattern of grants and subsidies available and regulation of proposed mergers between major companies. Some governments currently support major public works being undertaken by Private Finance Initiatives (PFI), which means private finance is provided for design, construction and operation of particular activities. The public body involved then may pay the private organisation involved a fee for providing the required service, the fee being calculated so as to reimburse the private organisation for any costs it has to bear and also for an agreed profit element. Alternatively the private organisation may be allowed to charge the public a fee, on a kind of franchise basis, for using the services involved. In such cases it is likely the sponsoring government body would be expected to indemnify the private organisation against any risks of making a loss. In many ways PFI projects are still at the experimental stage, there being considerable discussion about how the risks involved will be shared. Also projects proposed for funding by the PFI process have to be approved by the government. Even though the PFI contracts are still at the experimental stage, the British

TABLE 7.2 Some possible forms of central government management

Possible forms of management	Possible advantages and disadvantages
Just use staff on short-term contracts	*Advantages*: no long-term commitment to staff, staff easily adjusted to work load
	Disadvantages: no continuity of interest, valuable experience easily lost
Just have a small management team and all other work done by contractors	*Advantage*: easy to change workforce to match demand
	Disadvantage: contractors may need a lot of training. Contractors may not have all the contacts needed to do the job
Make top posts in departments open to election (these are management posts not political appointments)	*Advantage*: openly competitive. Top people not faceless civil servants
	Disadvantage: more elections, elected people may not have the necessary competence
Arrange for all members of staff to change departments every five years	*Advantage*: saves people only having narrow experience
	Disadvantage: no continuity, may need larger staff to allow for lost time due to changes
Arrange for all staff to spend every fifth year in private industry	*Advantage*: practical experience of other types of organisation
	Disadvantage: would generate need for extra staff, may be difficult to arrange suitable postings
Make all communications by teleworking	*Advantage*: if everything really effectively computerised it may be possible to reduce staff requirements
	Disadvantage: it may take a long time to introduce such a system
Restrict all record keeping to computerised record form	*Advantage*: space saving; easier access to records
	Disadvantages: complete stock of records could be lost, computer record may not be accepted or officially recorded
More fixed published criteria for all decisions	*Advantage*: easy to predict decisions
	Disadvantage: does not allow for special conditions that may exist

Government is contemplating planning the refurbishment of the Aldermaston Atomic Weapons Establishment on a PFI contract. The refurbishment contract is reported to be valued at £1 billion (Prynn 1999).

Having spent quite a lot of time examining the nature of the formal constraints on management and entrepreneurism in central government, I now want to move on to consider what changes could be made if it were possible to allow more initiative to be used. I want to consider use of initiative for generic improvements in the service given and not changes for change's sake. It is admitted that some changes can be beneficial just because restrictive practices do not thrive so well in new environments. Some of the changes possible have already been identified in Table 7.2, which also gives comment on the implications of change. The changes suggested might be considered outrageous but they are intended to stimulate critical thinking about possible developments. Only a limited range of advantages and disadvantages is given. It is left to the reader to explore just how extensive the advantages and disadvantages may be in real life.

Deciding how significant the advantages and disadvantages may be in real life is unlikely to be a simple matter. In many decisions the justification may just be based on conventions or even myths and legends. It is recognised that it may not be easy to quantify the value of advantages or disadvantages. But, as in all assessments of the value of activities that do not have an output directly measurable in money terms you have to start building up a picture of value by comparison with other activities. Care has to be taken to ensure that the comparison is made with activities that really do have similar characteristics. If the characteristics are not really similar the comparison can give very misleading results. The range of costs that are likely to have to be considered are summarised in Table 7.3. Costs should not be considered in isolation, some attempt should be made to include evaluation of the through life potential benefits. There are some very difficult problems to be dealt with in assessing benefits in money terms, so that they can be compared in a consistent way with costs. Some of the problems are identified in Table 7.4. It is sensible to assess the net benefit of an activity over the expected life of the activity, net benefit being the sum of benefits over the expected lifetime of the activity minus the sum of the costs over the expected lifetime. If the net benefit appears to be negative the value of the proposed activity would be very doubtful.

Assessing benefits and costs is not a precise form of analysis. It is, however, if used carefully, a useful guide to the possible net benefits. Some of the factors that may be the source of errors or uncertainty are listed in Table 7.5. The sources of error and uncertainty are not the same

TABLE 7.3 The range of costs that are likely to be considered in comparing the merits of various forms of civil service organisation

Cost element	Relevance
Staff costs (including pension)	This could be direct labour or contract labour
Office costs (including cleaning)	Either rent or purchase of office space (if there is considerable home working there could be a charge for renting home office)
Travel cost	Some travel costs must be allowed for – the amount of travel depends on the kind of work
Telephone/communication cost	Communication costs are inescapable
Furniture	The office will need some furniture designed for the specific kind of office involved
Equipment (computers and printers)	Most offices need some equipment, which must be kept up to date
Entertaining	Some entertaining is likely to be required, the amount required will depend on the purpose of the office
Accounts/finance (including contracts)	There will need to be some staff devoted to looking after the formal side of the organisation, from paying wages and bills to looking after contracts

for every activity. For example in assessment of a health service the cost of drugs may be an important variable whereas in modernising a railway system the cost of building new rolling stock and new routes may be the most important variables to consider. Further discussion of cost and benefit problems is given in Appendix 4.

Conclusions

Although it would be easy simply to endorse the view that management in central government organisations is management in a strait-jacket, such a view misses many of the subtle nuances of the role of central government. The essential character of central government management becomes clearer if it is considered to consist of two parts. One part is the operational part concerned simply with implementing legislation. The other part is concerned with advising ministers on the development of future policy and the changes that should be made to existing policy.

TABLE 7.4 A selection of the problems involved in assessing benefits

Activity	Benefits	Problem in assessing benefits in money terms
Build new motorway	Save time for road users Reduce accidents	Time saved can be costed and accidents can be costed in terms of reduced claims for accidents
Build new major specialist hospital	Faster treatment for people in the area, which would mean a better chance of recovery	The value of life saved and extended can be costed
Buy new fighter Buy new aircraft carrier Buy new tanks	To satisfy international defence obligations and to improve the nation's defence capability	These are generally more difficult benefits to cost. If there is a positive military threat the benefit could be costed in terms of the cost of gaining an advantage over the assumed threat
Build new town with its own industrial area	Improve the quality of living for new residents	The benefit could be measured in terms of the contribution the new town would make to the national GDP
Increase pensions	Improve the quality of life for the aged	The benefit could be taken as directly proportional to the increase in pension
Increase payments to European Union	To satisfy international obligations	This is a very difficult benefit to identify and quantify. In a crude way the benefit could be taken as the net receipts over payments

For the operational part of a central government organisation the constraints that it is subject to normally include: defining legislation, funding, staff, international commitments and agreements, political environment and emergencies. Some rationalisation of central government organisation has taken place under the guise of cuts in expenditure and some under the guise of privatisation.

TABLE 7.5 Some sources of errors and uncertainties in evaluating costs and benefits

Cost of benefit	Source of error/uncertainty	Comment
Cost	Inflation	Some costs may be subject to greater inflation than others
	Changes in interest rates	Particularly important when a large proportion of funding is borrowed
	Unexpected site/development costs	Some factors not allowed for in original plans may increase costs
	Availability of resources may change	It may become more expensive to obtain resources – wage/material costs may increase
	Taxes may change	Tax charge may change costs
Benefit	Potential benefits not fully identified	Benefit just measured by one factor not the whole spectrum of benefits
	Quantification of benefit may not be precise	This can destroy the whole basis for assessing benefits
	With time the perception of benefits may change	The longer the time-scale considered the more chance there is that the perception of benefits will change
	Comparison of benefits may be unsound	The benefits of a new military aeroplane are not directly comparable with the benefit of a new hospital or a new school

To a considerable extent the advisory function of the civil service is not constrained by legislation, in fact advice is expected to be unbiased and not constrained by conventions or past practices. In preparing advice the civil service may give consideration to the entrepreneurial factors involved. For example, building up advice on how privatisation could be used would involve consultation with many organisations including those representing industry. The final advice could represent a compromise between the views of the parties consulted. The advice would attempt to make it clear if the proposal would be successful in the entrepreneurial sense.

The basis on which judgements about the acceptability of such proposals are made often uses some form of cost-benefit analysis to aid the decision making process. It must be recognised that although cost-benefit analysis tools can be helpful they are not precise. When they are used some allowance must be made for possible errors and uncertainties. The sources of error and uncertainty include:

- Allowance for inflation

- Changes in interest rates which impact on the funding of the project

- Unexpected site/development costs give rise to claims for additional payments

- Availability of resources may change and give rise to uncertainties about the outcome of the project

- Taxes may change and change the whole basis of costing

- Potential benefits may not be fully identified and quantification of benefits may be wrong resulting in the net value of the proposal being uncertain

- With time perception of benefits may change, this may undermine the acceptability of the proposition

- Comparison of benefits may be unsound, this would undermine the assessment of acceptability and the whole decision making process

References

The Civil Service Yearbook (1998), London: The Stationery Office, p. CXViii and editorial.

The Government Response to the Deregulation Task Force Report 1996 (1997) London: Cabinet Office.

'An inspector calls . . . and another' (1999) *Daily Telegraph* 17 May, p. 31.

Jenkins, K., Caines, K. and Jackson, A. (1988) *Improving Management in Government: The Next Steps*, a report by the Efficiency Unit to the Prime Minster, London: Her Majesty's Stationery Office, pp. 3, 4, 13–16, 31–2

Lake, H. (1999) 'Little one can do when an inspector calls', *The Times* 18 May, p. 24.

Inspector at the Door (1999) London: Federation of Small Businesses.

Prynn, J. (1999) 'PFI to rebuild atomic site in £1 billion deal', *Evening Standard* 8 February, p. 33.

CHAPTER EIGHT

The reality of management and entrepreneurism in the private sector

As has been hinted in Chapters 6 and 7 the motivation in the private sector is quite different to that in either central or local government organisations. In very simple terms the aim in the private sector is to help the company grow in the most profitable way possible, while in the government sector the main concern is to satisfy its political masters and statutory obligations. Although the motivation in each type of sector is quite different there are areas of similarity which include recruitment, training and contracting. Also there are many interfaces between local and central government organisations and private sector organisations, which means that each party has to behave in a way that is compatible with the other. One of the very important interfaces is when a private sector organisation is supplying a government organisation with some goods or services.

A company in the private sector does not have some God-given right to stay in business, nor is its existence protected by legislation. Funding for future development has to be earned and income has to be greater than expenditure. This may sound very trite but it is an inescapable truth for life in the private sector.

In general, decision making in the private sector is faster than in the government sector. This is mainly due to the private sector not having to get approval from elected members and other government bodies before a decision is made. There are of course cases where decision making in private industry is as slow as in government bodies, this is particularly true in cases where private industry is negotiating a major government contract. For example, a company negotiating a contract to design and build a new fighter aeroplane may be involved in years of negotiation on such factors as: definition of specification, whether or not the work should be undertaken by an international consortium or just nationally and how many aeroplanes are to be bought. An example of just how long the process may be is given by the fact that in 1999 the US Air Force issued a contract for a study of the concepts for a strike aircraft to replace B-1, B-2, and B-52 bombers after 2030 (*Aerospace International* 1999: 9). The options to be considered included whether the aircraft should be subsonic, supersonic, hypersonic, manned or unmanned. So from concept to production of aircraft entering squadron service can take 30 years.

In a very similar way negotiating contracts with international bodies or consortia may take a considerable time. A company has to decide if getting involved in such government funded type contracts yields an adequate return on the resources that have to be deployed. The question of assessing the acceptability of projects is discussed further in Appendix 3.

In the private sector entrepreneurism is the driving force behind all activity. No manager in any part of a private sector organisation can be considered satisfactory unless he/she ensures that all activities they get involved with make a positive contribution to improving the efficiency of the organisation. In a small company it is easy for everyone to see the relationship between sales, costs and available income. In large companies it is possible for whole departments to be isolated from involvement in balancing sales, income and costs. It is accepted that for some activities it may be difficult to quantify the contribution to improving efficiency. In the following, consistent ways of assessing the value of improvements are developed.

The range of entrepreneurial factors managers have to consider in the private sector is indicated in Table 8.1. The importance given to each factor will vary from company to company and department to department. In a small specialised department in a large company the range of factors considered may be very small, but a manager of a large concern is likely to have a very large range of factors to consider. The factors considered in the table are mainly related to some kind of manufacturing activity but it is easy to relate them to any other type of activity. For example the product could be insurance policies or loans or consultancy reports or research projects completed. In a large company there is likely to be an active research department and it is sometimes difficult to ensure that a research department's resources are used efficiently.

In some ways the success of management and entrepreneurism in the private sector could be described as depending upon identifying all the risks involved and reducing them to an acceptable level. The question of risk assessment is dealt with at length in Chicken (1996).

An entrepreneur must assess both the risk factors that are internal to the organisation and those that are external to the organisation. Table 8.2 sets out the basis for assessment of major internal risk factors that should

TABLE 8.1 Summary of entrepreneurial factors to be considered by managers in the private sector

Factor	Implications
Market demand	Is the size of the market known with precision?
Product designed for market	Is the current design of product what the market wants? Has the design to be changed in the near future?
Production capacity	Is production capacity adequate to satisfy demand? What changes in capacity are likely to be needed in future?
Market price compared with production costs	Does the market price give an adequate profit margin over total production costs?
Staff requirements	Are all the suitably trained staff likely to be required in post?
Regulations to be satisfied	What government regulations will have to be satisfied and how can it be shown they are satisfied?
Adequacy of finance available	Are all the funds required for future development of the company available or has greater funding to be found?
Future finance requirements	Are sources of future finance identified and likely to be adequate?
Possible crises to be allowed for	What possible crises have to be considered? They may include: strikes, loss of contracts, bad payers, riots and wars.
Raw material availability	Are supplies of raw material likely to be lost without warning and what alternatives are likely to be available?
Staff training requirements	Do staff need training to deal effectively with current and future problems?
Competition	Is there strong market competition that is likely to lead to a reduction in share of the market? How faithful are customers likely to be? What ways are there of keeping them faithful?

be considered and Table 8.3 sets out the basis for assessment of external factors that should be considered. Attention is drawn to the fact that socio-political factors are considered in both tables. The reason for this is that there are elements of socio-political factors peculiar to both internal and external risk factors.

TABLE 8.2 Summary of the basis for assessment of internal risk factors

Major risk factor area	Possible basis for assessment of risk acceptability	Comment on assessment
Economic	1. Analysis of supply and demand characteristics	– The object being to determine the implications for the organisation.
	2. Cost analysis	– Prediction of cost should be as precise as possible but the magnitude of the uncertainty should be recognised.
	3. Future capital requirements	– Amount of capital should be identified.
	4. Five and ten-year plan for organisation	– This needs the results of assessments against the first three criteria. But with respect to cost analysis and future capital requirements, there would have to be iterative development.
Technical	1. Product acceptability review	– The product review should show what research and development is required to satisfy future market requirements.
	2. Research and development plan	– Has to be tailored to meet what are seen as future market requirements.
Socio-Political	1. Human resource review 2. Assessment of organisational structure 3. Training programme	– Assessment of these factors will show what action has to be taken to ensure that human resources are available and organised in a way that will enable an organisation to satisfy future requirements.
	4. Security review	– The security arrangements of an organisation must be such that they ensure risks are kept to a minimum.
	5. Assessment of public relations status	– Relations with the public must be kept harmonious to ensure that any opposition to an organisation is kept to a minimum.

TABLE 8.3   Summary of the basis for assessment of external risk factors

Major risk factor area	Possible basis for assessment of risk acceptability	Comment on assessment
Economic	1. Is the size of market changing? 2. Are there new operators in the market? 3. What new markets are developing?	– With a product that changes little over the years it may be possible to identify long-term trends in the market. This would be more difficult with novel products.
	4. Where is the economy currently in the trade cycle?	– Monitoring relevant data gives a fair indication of trends.
	5. How are interest and exchange rates changing?	– Within what range are rates likely to change.
	6. What is the availability of additional capital?	– What costs are associated with making more capital available.
	7. Are there problems with cash flow?	– Important changes are apparent quite quickly.
Technical	1. Can the product be improved, to be better than the competition's?	– Forces for change must be recognised and acted upon.
	2. Is there an alternative product on the market that is better?	– Can the producer of the alternative be bought?
	3. Are competitor's production processes better?	– If they are better can they be adopted?
	4. Are additional safety and environmental regulations likely to be introduced that will be difficult to satisfy?	– Ignoring such changes can be expensive in the long run.
	5. Are there problems with external suppliers for current and future products?	– Problems with suppliers can be expensive and damaging to a company.
Socio-Political	1. What changes in the law are imminent and how will they affect this organisation? 2. Are there any public relations problems that have to be overcome? 3. Are there any security problems such as exposure to theft, fraud and terrorism that have to be overcome? 4. Are there any political problems that could affect the operation of the organisation?	– These problems cannot always be predicted. But the nature of them shows how important it is to carefully monitor trends and events outside an organisation.

Some of the risk factors such as technical factors are fairly hard, that is they can be assessed in quantitative terms. Other factors like socio-political factors are soft, that is they have to be judged in subjective qualitative terms.

To arrive at an overall assessment of the acceptability of the risks involved usually some form of risk ranking is used. The overall risk is the sum of the ranking of the risk of all the individual components of the proposition.

The six essential steps in assessing the acceptability of a future line of development in the private sector are:

1   Identify the proposals to be considered.

2   Identify the features of the proposals that have to be considered.

3   Determine the criteria by which the merit/demand of each feature of a proposal can be judged.

4   Determine the time-scale over which the various merits/demands involved can be judged.

5   For each project evaluate in a consistent way the merits/demands of the various features involved.

6   Using the results of the evaluation of merits/demands determine which proposal deserves the highest priority for being adopted.

There is further discussion of the problems of determining strategy and priority in Chicken and Hayns (1999). To illustrate the essential features of the methodology in the following, three hypothetical cases are considered. Although the cases are hypothetical they are built on an amalgam of real life cases. The three cases are: an aircraft component maker trying to get a major order, an insurance company trying to improve its premium/claims ratio and a construction company undertaking the principal contractor role in a major road construction programme.

Description of case 1

A major aircraft component maker trying to get a major order

The company has been manufacturing hydraulic components and systems for the aircraft industry for 75 years. The components made range from hydraulic pumps to fuel pumps and from fuel systems to undercarriages. The products have to be designed to satisfy the strict performance specification laid down by the aircraft designer and the regulatory bodies. Due to a downturn in the market for military aircraft, which was not offset by an increase in orders for civil aircraft, the company was faced with having more workers and capacity than it needed.

The company is in the process of tendering for a very large contract to supply hydraulic systems and undercarriages for a new design of civil airliner being developed by an international consortium of companies. The structure of the consortium is complex consisting of a mixture of state and private industries, the organisation being brought together by an intergovernment treaty. The treaty specifies what proportion of the work should go to each of the participating countries. This means that each supplier has to compete on price within the official constraint of a limited possible share of the market.

In this situation the company saw it was faced with six options, five of which involved decisions by other parties. The options are summarised in Table 8.4.

On the assumption that the owners want to stay in the same business they are faced with five options: bid the lowest price, adjust bid so that it does not infringe quotas, take over a similar company in one of the other participating countries, complete diversification into another industry and partly diversity into another industry. Assuming that the company's main aims are to maximise the profit it makes, to stay in business and if possible to expand the business, then as the market for aircraft components is not seen as an expanding market it might be the view of the board that the long-term aims of the company are best served by diversifying into other markets. This could take the form of developing new products or taking over a company operating in another industry.

So far the discussion has been in subjective qualitative terms. Ideally the options should be assessed in objective quantitative terms. Such an assessment for a large project might take the form of risk assessments involving assessment of perhaps several hundred factors. An explanation of the basic methodology is given in Chapter 4, Appendix 3 and Chicken and Haynes (1999). An odd number of rating points has been adopted to show the implications of using such a scale. The form of the assessment procedure is shown in Table 8.5. In Table 8.6 the assessment procedure is applied to case 1 and shows that selling the company and reinvesting the money is likely to yield the best entrepreneurial result. Taking over a company in another country is likely to be the second best option. Diversifying into another industry is likely to give the worst entrepreneurial result.

TABLE 8.4   Summary of options facing case 1 company

Option	Origin of option	Implications
1. Bid is lowest price and does not infringe quota.	Bid based on company's knowledge of the market and knowledge of its costs.	The company concentrates on developing its current range of products. Labour force unchanged. New machines introduced as funding becomes available.
2. Bid infringes quota so all work bid for not obtained.	Original intergovernment agreement laid down quota scheme.	Labour force might have to be reduced as all work required might not be obtained. Alternative considered, join with a contractor in another country and qualify for a larger share of the contracts.
3. Before making a bid, take over a similar company in another country that is also part of the consortium.	This option may be proposed by the company's own board.	Some difficulty in integrating a company with a different culture. May not require all current labour force. There may be some government objection on the grounds that a monopoly is being formed.
4. Complete diversification into another industry.	An option also proposed by the company's own board.	Diversification into another industry takes a considerable time and requires funds for new equipment and training staff.
5. Partly diversify into another industry.	An option also proposed by the company's own board.	This may be quicker and involve less risk than competitor diversification.
6. Sell the company.	An option also proposed by the company's own board.	This would leave investors with money in their hands but no further interest in the company's activities.

TABLE 8.5 The entrepreneurial rating of options

Entrepreneurial rating = potential return × likelihood of success

Potential return	Rating
Large negative return	5
Small negative return	4
Zero return	3
Small positive return	2
Large positive return	1

Likelihood of success	Rating
Success unlikely	5
Possibility of success needs more analysis	4
Success uncertain	3
Success possible	2
Success likely	1

Entrepreneurial rating

Rating	Decision
16–25	Proposal unacceptable
10–15	Serious doubts about proposal
6–9	Proposal marginally acceptable
3–5	Possibly adequate nature
1–2	Good return on investment likely

TABLE 8.6 Entrepreneurial rating of options in case 1

Option	Potential return	Likelihood of success	Entrepreneurial rating
Low bid not infringing quota	2	2	4
Bid infringes quota so not all work bid for obtained	2	2	4
Company takes over company in another country before bid is made	1	2	2
Diversify into another industry	4	3	12
Partly diversify into another industry	2	2	4
Sell the company (cash re-invested)	1	1	1

Description of case 2

An insurance company trying to improve its premium/claims ratio

A large insurance company dealing with non-life risks, that is mainly business, plant and equipment risks, has found that in the last three years claims have increased to the extent they are nearly equal to premium income. If allowed to continue, this state of affairs could develop into a situation that would threaten the very existence of the company. When claims are greater than premium income the company has to draw on reserves, a situation that by definition can only last for as long as the reserves last.

The claims have been mainly related to computers and computer-controlled equipment. There are six options the company has to assess: (1) stop taking computer-related business; (2) increase premiums; (3) increase the range of policies it offers; (4) take over another company with a different range of policy products; (5) sell the company; (6) reduce the range of claims covered. The options are considered and summarised in Table 8.7, and assessed using the same form of assessment used in case 1 and shown in Table 8.5. The result of the assessment of the options is presented in Table 8.8.

The analysis showed that option 4, taking over another company with a different range of policy products, and option 5, selling the company, had the greatest likelihood of yielding a return. Option 6, reducing the range of risks covered, was the least likely to yield a return.

Description of case 3

A construction company undertaking the role of principal contractor in a major road construction programme

In Britain, in construction work the term principal contractor has a very special meaning, which is specified in the Health and Safety Construction, Design and Management Regulations (The CDM Regulations 1996). It means the lead contractor for the project is the contractor to whom all the other contractors and sub-contractors are responsible. The regulations firmly define the principal contractor as having sole responsibility for and control of all activities on site.

TABLE 8.7 Summary of options facing case 2 company

Option	Origin of option	Implications
1. Stop taking computer-related business.	Assessment of the pattern of premium/ claims and just deal directly with the cause.	This might reduce the company's prospects for growth.
2. Increase premiums.	A direct way of improving the premium/claim balance but ignores the impact on the volume of business.	Unless other companies also increase their premiums the company could lose business.
3. Increase the range of policies sold.	The essential aim being to increase the volume of business.	Could increase business.
4. Take over another company with a different range of policy products.	A way of expanding the business and perhaps a way of improving efficiency.	Could also increase turnover.
5. Sell company	A way of converting assets to cash.	It could leave investors with money in their hands but no further interest in the company's future.
6. Reduce the range of risks covered.	Just a financial manoeuvre to improve profit margins.	This would leave clients taking a greater share of the risks.

TABLE 8.8 Entrepreneurial rating of the options in case 2

Option	Potential return	Likelihood of success	Entrepreneurial rating
1. Stop taking computer-related business.	3	2	6
2. Increase premiums.	2	2	4
3. Increase the range of policies sold.	2	2	4
4. Take over another company with a different range of policy products.	1	1	1
5. Sell company.	1	1	1
6. Reduce range of risks covered.	3	3	9

The principal contractor has to commit considerable resources to ensure that a project is completed on time and to the required specification. Although there are several ways a project can be financed, in this case the project is financed directly by the government with a date set for completion and a fixed price for the work. The payment for the work has to be made against monthly invoices for work done during the previous month. No allowance has been made in the contract for payments beyond the fixed budget.

The project is half complete and although 12 invoices have been issued only one payment has been received. The work done so far has involved the contractor in having to deal with some difficult geo-technical problems that were not envisaged at the time the contract was signed. This has resulted in the contractor making a claim for a variation of the contract price.

The problems the contractor is faced with are:

1   Financing operations when 11 months of invoices are unpaid.

2   Getting the client to adjust the contract price to allow for the difficulties encountered.

3   Getting the client to agree to a revision of the completion date set in the contract.

4   Should work be stopped while negotiations with the client go on about contract revision and late payments?

Following the same form of analysis as used for cases 1 and 2, Table 8.9 summarises the options open to the contractor.

The entrepreneurial rating was calculated on the same basis as cases 1 and 2 and the results are shown in Table 8.10. The two best entrepreneurial ratings were found to be arrange extra funding from financial institutions and carry on working on the assumption that financial problems will be solved in the contractor's favour. The two worst entrepreneurial ratings were withdraw from the contract and declare the company bankrupt.

Analysis of the results of the three case studies

The three cases considered were three very different kinds of cases from the private sector, but together they make a fairly representative sample of

TABLE 8.9 Summary of options open to the contractor in case 3

Option	Origin of option	Implication
1. Withdraw from contract.	Company decision when it could see a risk of making a loss.	This removes the chance of profit.
2. Arrange extra funding from financial institutions.	Company decision to try to stay in business.	Extra interest may reduce profit. Time to arrange funding may delay completion of project.
3. Take legal action against client for late payment and additional costs.	Company attempt to force client into action.	Time for legal process may delay completion and increase costs.
4. Declare the company bankrupt.	A stop loss decision by company.	May save investors further losses but eliminates chance of profit.
5. Carry on working on the assumption that financial problems will be settled in the contractor's favour.	A company decision based on the optimistic assumption that everything will eventually be all right.	May produce a profit.
6. Bring in a partner to share the problems and profits if any.	A company option to share problems.	Share risks and profits. Takes time to arrange.

TABLE 8.10 Entrepreneurial rating of the options in case 3

Option	Potential return	Likelihood of success	Entrepreneurial rating
1. Withdrawal from contract.	5	5	25
2. Arrange extra funding from financial institutions.	2	1	2
3. Take legal action against client for late payment and additional costs.	2	2	4
4. Declare the company bankrupt.	5	5	25
5. Carry on working on the assumption that financial problems will be settled in the contractor's favour.	1	2	2
6. Bring in a partner to share the problems and profits, if any.	2	2	4

private sector activities. The options considered are a fairly small sample of the options that would be considered in real life. However, the sample is large enough to illustrate the range of options that have to be considered and the validity of the methodology. The analysis was made on the basis of subjective qualitative data and as such is subject to all the uncertainties associated with the use of such data. If reliable quantitative data is available the uncertainty associated with the analysis can be reduced.

The methodology of building an entrepreneurial rating for each option gives the decision maker a logically defensible and transparent way of assessing the acceptability of the options open. As demonstrated the methodology does not give any indication of the uncertainty associated with the rating. One elementary qualitative approach to assessing the significance of uncertainty is to assess the impact on the entrepreneurial rating of the potential return and the likelihood of the success rating being increased by one digit or decreased by one digit.

Conclusions

Management in the private sector has, in making any decision, to take into account the impact of the decision on the entrepreneurial strength of the organisation involved. A useful aid to assessing such options involves the entrepreneurial rating methodology, which was demonstrated in the assessment of cases 1, 2 and 3.

The assessment of the three cases clearly exposed the difference in the type of decisions that have to be taken by management in the private sector. The special feature of management in the private sector is that their action can determine the future and fate of their organisation, an option not open to managers in the public sector who at all times are subject to the constraints of the legislation under which they function.

In assessing the acceptability of options available the decision maker has to determine which of the options is likely to have the potential for the largest positive return and the highest likelihood of success.

The range of factors that have to be considered by managers making private sector decisions includes:

- Market demand

- Product design for market

- Production capacity

- Market price compared with production costs

- Staff requirements

- Regulations to be satisfied

- Adequacy of finance available

- Future finance requirements

- Possible crises to be allowed for

- Raw material availability

- Staff training requirements

- Competition

References

Aerospace International (1999) published by the Royal Aeronautical Society, London, October: p. 9

Chicken, J.C. (1996) *Risk Handbook*, London: International Thomson Business Press, pp. 122–51.

Chicken, J.C. and Hayns, M.R. (1999) *Strategy and Priority*, London: International Thomson Business Press.

The CDM (Construction, Design and Management) Regulations (1996), London: Her Majesty's Stationery Office.

CHAPTER NINE

Where improvement in management efficiency can be made

In absolute terms nothing is perfect, improvements can always be made. Before examining where improvements in management efficiency can be made you to have to be certain what the particular managers are expected to do. Generally the role of management is directed towards ensuring that an organisation's aims are satisfied. To prevent any misunderstanding about the way the word manager is used in the following, its use must be explained. The term manager is used in this book in a very particular way. It is used to denote the person or group of people who are responsible for running and developing the organisation. Such people are sometimes referred to as directors, chief executives or even partners in some types of organisation. In the armed forces they would be officers of senior rank. In a privately owned company the owner may also be the top director, with other members of the family fitted in at other positions in the organisation.

Management is, except in very small organisations, rarely a single unified body. It is more usually a set of disparate units each with their own specialised function. This also means that there is a hierarchy of managers each with a special role. In Table 9.1 the nature of the various types of managers in the hierarchy is summarised. It is stressed that recognition of the existence of management hierarchies is not intended to endorse the existence of hierarchies. The view is supported that the number of levels of management should be kept as small and as simple as possible.

Usually the work to be done has to be divided into sub-tasks that are within the operational competence and capability of the subsidiary units or people. In a small organisation the whole organisation may be run by just one or two people. In all cases the basic aim is the same, it is just the scale of the operation that is different. The tasks and sub-tasks to be done have to be identified and the time-scales for completion and target costs have to be set. It is then management's central task to ensure that tasks are completed on time and to budget. Targets are unlikely to be met unless the whole task is properly understood and any interference with completion eliminated. To ensure targets set are realistically achievable with the resources that can be made available, it is essential that the managers responsible for targets being achieved are involved in the process of setting the targets. It is also vital that at the beginning of any project the resources required are: fully identified, carefully selected and their availability confirmed. It is important that the resources are available at the time they are required so the project can be completed in the most efficient way possible. This requirement applies to any type of project whether it is developing a new aeroplane or establishing a new department in a government organisation.

There are many important aspects about the selection of resources that must not be overlooked. If a business aims to be ahead of the competition it must have the most appropriate equipment and people with the required pattern of high-quality skills. This is not a task that has only to be done once, all aspects of resources have to be kept under review. People's skills become outdated, equipment becomes obsolete and manufacturing processes change. Table 9.2 gives a summary of some of the dramatic technical changes that have taken place in recent years. These changes have had a tremendous impact on the whole of society, including management. It is very unlikely that there will be less dramatic technical changes in the future.

If unexpected problems arise it is management's responsibility to ensure that the problems are solved. It is an important responsibility of management to ensure that when problems are identified the lines of communication are such that information about problems passes without delay to those able to solve them and redesign plans if necessary. This requirement implies that everyone involved knows their role exactly and has the initiative to take appropriate action.

The ability to recognise and solve problems quickly and effectively requires a deep understanding of the process involved, sufficient knowledge and leadership to take action quickly and effectively. Dithering and waiting for the proposed action to be blessed by everyone is likely to amplify delays, magnify the problems involved and increase costs.

The comments already made begin to expose the importance of the element of leadership in management. Even the professional working alone has to show leadership in the way his/her professional activities are conducted. For example a medical doctor has to show leadership in convincing a sick patient of the treatment that should be accepted. Similarly a lawyer has to show leadership in presenting a case in court.

TABLE 9.1 The nature of the role of managers in a medium-sized firm

Level	Nature	Function
Top	Overall responsibility, no part of the organisation is outside his/her responsibilities.	To ensure a realistic strategy for the long-term future of the organisation is developed, kept to and adapted to changing circumstances.
Proximate top	Answers to the top manager and is responsible to the top manager.	To act as deputy for the top manager and to provide any technical or administrative support required.
Middle	May just be responsible for a department such as firm's production or sales. Any alteration to function has to be agreed with either the top manager or the proximate manager.	To ensure that the department he/she is responsible for is operated as efficiently as possible and satisfies the aims set for it.
Primary	Functions just at the basic operational level. Main role is to ensure that operational targets are met.	To ensure plans laid down by the top manager are kept to.

TABLE 9.2 A summary of the dramatic technical changes in recent years

Change	Implications
Motor car	Fast transport
Aeroplanes	Very fast travel and transport
Photocopiers	Fast copying
Automation	Fast production with fewer workers
Lasers	Precise measurement, location and outlining
New medical drugs	People live longer, changes in the structure of society
Mobile phones	Fast communications
Computers	Data analysis faster, information more easily available, growth in knowledge management; new ways of doing business
New materials	Stronger, lighter, more durable materials available

A professional engineer presenting a design to a client has to show leadership in justifying the design. Another important aspect of leadership is motivating a team. Although motivation is a word that is bandied about in discussion of team management as though you just have to say the word and motivation instantly develops, in practice a lot of care has to be taken in building a motivated team. Construction of a motivated team requires careful selection of the members of the team and provision of an appropriate working environment.

There is no unique way of motivating a team, the approach to motivation has to be tailored to suit the activity the team is involved with. It is easy to understand the difference between motivating a football team, a commando regiment, an airliner crew, an insurance office staff and a hospital operating theatre team. In each case a different range of skills and working procedures are involved, also the members of the various types of team have different expectations. It is important to allow for differences in expectations and where possible to show team members how they can achieve their expectations. Also it has to be made clear that some expectations may be unrealistic.

In providing leadership the manager involved has to understand and ensure that every effort is made to satisfy an organisation's overall strategy and priorities. A major effort that management has to make is translating and explaining to operational teams the nature of the organisation's strategy and priority and what they mean in terms of real targets that have to be satisfied.

The aims of leadership can be summed up as providing, as efficiently as possible, a sense of partnership and direction towards achieving particular clearly defined objectives.

Leadership is not the only function of management, other important functions of management are summarised in Table 9.3.

Management is not some abstract activity carried out by some humanoid robot or automaton, hopefully it is carried out by trained people capable of independent thought and with an enquiring mind. This of course assumes that the process of selecting managers has been done in a systematic and rigorous way, with the selection process being tailored to match the type of management function to be performed. For example, the process for selecting an office manager would be rather different from selecting an airline pilot or a brain surgeon. Further discussion of the problems of selecting managers is given in Appendix 1. The possible selection methods range from a simple interview to a complex set of tests including psychometric and physical capability tests. An important way of improving management performance is to improve the quality of managers.

TABLE 9.3 The functions of management

Function	Scope of implementation
Target setting	Must be clear about what has to be achieved and the resources required and available.
Problem solving	Must recognise the spectrum of problems that may arise and the solutions that may be appropriate. Possible solutions should identify the magnitude of the risk associated with each option.
Leadership	Generating confidence, team building and ensuring competence and capability to achieve targets efficiently.
Team building	Ensuring good responsive communications and that everyone knows what is expected of them including the action that has to be taken if problems arise.
Dealing with emergencies	Ensure a damage limitation plan exists and effective arrangements are made for work to continue as soon as possible.

If you are going to introduce some improvements, a way of measuring the effectiveness of the improvements is required. Ideally the measurement should be quantitative, as qualitative measures of improvement lack precision and tend to contain a large element of emotional judgement. Where a production process or a commercial operation is involved it is easy to see how a quantitative measure of the value of the improvement can be developed. The problem of measuring the effectiveness of improvements for non-price activities is more difficult, as there is difficulty in defining the parameter that should be used as a measure of efficiency and deciding how the parameter should be measured. Even measuring improvements in terms of cost and benefits generally lacks precision due to the uncertainty associated with quantifying benefits. The benefits of some state provided services are particularly hard to justify and many of the methods proposed, even those proposed officially, do little more than rate benefits on the basis of expert opinion.

In Table 9.4 possible ways of measuring improvements for a range of activities are summarised. The list of activities considered is not intended to be comprehensive but merely to indicate the range of parameters that may be used to measure management performance. In practice for any particular activity a combination of parameters may be needed to measure performance. However, the table does give a very good starting point for discussion of where improvements in management efficiency can be made.

TABLE 9.4 Possible ways of measuring improvement in management performance in a range of activities

Type of activity	Activity	Possible ways of measuring improvements in management
Commercial private industry	Manufacturing industry	Production increased at lower cost and improved quality.
	Retail industry	Sales and profit margins increased.
	Banking	Profits increased – loan defaults reduced.
	Insurance	Premiums increased and claims reduced.
	Consultancy	Consultancy fee income increased and client portfolio increased.
	Transport	Number of passengers carried increased and profits increased.
State-controlled organisation	Civil service	Costs kept within budget and government satisfied with performance.
	Local government	Government and local community satisfied with performance.
	National health service	General health of nation improved, quality of life for the sick improved.
	Education	Examination results improved, quality raised to that of advanced countries.
	Social services	Community and government satisfied with service.
	Government agencies operating on a commercial basis	Improvement in profits and growth in services provided.
	Development of industry, science and technology	Per head of population more new technologies being developed and profitably exploited in advance of other countries.

The process of measuring performance and efficiency is an important management tool as it identifies where improvements can be made.

In the following, possible improvements in management efficiency are postulated in each of the activities identified in Table 9.4. The conclusion that seems to be justified from the table is that lower cost and higher quality are indicators of higher efficiency, common to all activities, and they show where management action is likely to result in improvements in overall efficiency. Now to consider in more detail possible improvements in each of the activities mentioned in Table 9.4.

Manufacturing industry

Like all commercial activities the aim will be to increase the share of the market or create a new market. Increasing the share of the market can only be achieved by reaching the market at a lower cost, and/or a higher quality. In some cases the required acceptable quality may be set by the customer. The way in which costs may be reduced depends on the type of industry. But, whatever the industry, low cost high quality production is likely to depend on having high quality machines and equipment, high quality raw material and well-trained staff to use the machines. Also, where components have to be bought in from outside, it is vital that the supplier provides a product that satisfies customers' requirements on time. The importance of producing products of a quality that satisfies the customer is an essential requirement of maintaining and increasing a market share. An appropriate quality control is not just a question of inspecting the final product – it requires the whole organisation to adopt a quality-conscious work culture. This means the quality of every operation has to be checked, from specifying raw materials to testing that the end product satisfies the customer's specification. There is further discussion of the role of quality assurance in Appendix 2.

Retail industry

In the retail industry, perhaps more than in any other industry, weekly sales figures give a good indication of the extent to which what is being offered satisfies the market demand. Again quality and price are important indicators of performance, but also the way the goods are presented has an important influence on sales. Another important factor in the retail trade is fashion. Fashion does not just apply to clothes, it also applies to food, cars, television sets, houses and even machines. In fact it is difficult to think of an item in the retail market that would not be influenced, to some extent, by fashion. Examples of the way markets change are: the market for black and white television sets has to a large extent been displaced by colour sets; similarly not many cars are now sold without power steering or catalytic converters. This suggests that another way of judging the efficiency of a retail business could be its capability of adapting the range of goods sold to the changing market and at the same time increasing turnover.

Banking

As with the retail trade banking has to adapt to the changing needs of its customers and to changing technology. Many transactions are now carried out without the customer entering the bank. Money is drawn from a hole in the wall and many transactions are done by telephone, fax and e-mail. The number of branches and banks is falling. The range of services a bank offers is now much more than simple banking, it includes insurance, loans, car finance and house purchase mortgages, sale of pensions and the buying and selling of stocks and shares. A very good index of a bank's efficiency is the dividend it can afford to pay. Banks with many bad loans are likely to have to draw on their reserves, reduce the dividend they pay or even go bankrupt.

Insurance

A very simple way the insurance industry prospers is if premium income is higher than claims. It is recognised that premiums may not always be in phase with claims. There may be one year when due to a series of natural disasters claims are higher than premiums, but averaged over three years premiums are higher than claims. Efficiency of the industry can be judged by the way premium income and the margin over claims increase over a period of several years. This suggests that management can be judged to be more efficient if it increases premium income and reduces the total claims. As the present market for insurance is fairly well covered insurers are, even more than usual, looking for new risks to cover and ways of reducing claims. The range of risks people want insurance cover for expands as technology expands and as the standard of living improves. The better the risk is understood the more precisely it will be possible to specify an appropriate premium. This leads to the conclusion that in the insurance industry management efficiency can be assessed by the way they deal with the risks they accept and the extent to which they keep claims below premiums income.

Consultancy

It is very difficult to determine how improvements can be made in the efficiency of consultancy management. By the very nature of consultancies they exist to satisfy the needs of their clients. It may be that a client asks a consultancy to undertake a particular task in a way that is not the most efficient. This means that the product of a consultancy may not be the best. In such cases the consultant must, as a matter of professional integrity, make clear to the client that they are not asking for the most efficient solution to their problem. As a consultancy does not necessarily produce the most efficient product some other way of measuring the efficiency of consulting management must be found. Two other measures of efficiency are: (1) total turnover; and (2) profit/employee. Of the two measures profit/employee is preferred as it gives a measure of the efficiency of each employee and it provides a basis for comparing the efficiency of one consultancy with another. Such comparisons are only valid if like consultancies are compared. Misleading results are obtained if the performance of a leather consultancy is compared with a Formula 1 racing car design consultancy.

Transport

With privately owned transport companies the efficiency of the operations may be measured by the dividend paid or the return on investment. Judgement of the efficiency of transport operations where government subsidies are given is more difficult. International comparisons can give an indication of the comparative efficiency.

State-controlled organisations

The state-controlled activities identified in Table 9.4 are considered together as the factors controlling their efficiency are such that they have much more in common with one another than the factors controlling commercial private industries' efficiency. The two dominant factors are budget and political policy. Civil service/local government/national health service and education departments have, like all other government-funded activities, to operate within budgets that are set centrally. To a very large extent state organisations do not operate in a way that is very sensitive to the market, that is to the public, in the same way that a commercial organisation has to do. What they provide is set and limited by legislation. Certainly elected members have to follow political party policies and be sensitive to the views of the people that have elected them, but the speed of response of a state organisation to a public demand is very much slower than a commercial organisation's response to its market conditions. Even election promises are a very doubtful guide to what will happen. In many ways state organisations have more the characteristics of a dictatorship than a commercial organisation. Activities are further complicated by the role that spin doctors play in presenting facts about the operation of state organisations. No matter how they are dressed up spin doctors play the role of propaganda operators dressing up facts in a way that makes them look attractive. Propaganda, no matter what it is called, is an essential feature of dictatorships.

Against the background of spin doctoring how can the real efficiency of management in the state sector be judged? Simply keeping within budget is an inadequate measure of efficiency of a state organisation. Satisfaction of the public is not something that can be measured consistently with precision in every case. For example the view may be expressed that privatisation of some central and local functions will give maximum efficiency, the view being expressed without being supported by a critical assessment of the proposition. While it is possible that in some cases privatisation may improve efficiency there are many cases in which the improvements may not be as great or as real as suggested in political debates on the subject.

In Table 9.5 an outline is given of the potential advantages and disadvantages of privatisation of some state organisations.

While it is possible to see that in some cases there may be advantages in privatisation it is not a practical solution in every case. The cases that are more likely to benefit from privatisation are those in

TABLE 9.5 Advantages and disadvantages of privatisation of state organisations

Type of organisation	Potential advantages of privatisation	Potential disadvantages of privatisation
Advising on policy developments	Free from pressures brought on by existing state organisations.	Might not have access to all relevant information. State organisation would need to retain a team to monitor performance of the privatised unit. Privatised unit may find it difficult to deal with the variable work load associated with dealing with a state organisation.
An organisation whose activity is factory-like production, e.g. books, equipment, aeroplanes, electricity	Frees the organisation from some bureaucratic controls. Allows the organisation to exploit market potential. Allows organisation to develop new products.	If privatisation is complete the state loses control of the activity. If privatisation is only partial, that is the state retains some control, the state needs to retain some staff to monitor performance.
An organisation that has some national security role	Cost saving.	Not possible to give a private organisation responsibility for an activity that has to be responsible directly to the head of state. Would need a lot of staff to control activity.
An organisation that is responsible to the government for gathering intelligence of a confidential nature	Cost saving.	It is unlikely that a government's interests in confidentiality could be adequately protected if it was privatised.

which the activities involved resemble a factory operation that supplies a free market. Activities that are likely to involve a high degree of confidentiality of government information are cases that are not easily made suitable for privatisation.

Where privatisation is not 100 per cent, there are constraints on the partly privatised organisation so the gain in efficiency is not likely to be as great as it could be. In some cases emotional and political feelings run very high and the response to these feelings may dictate that another solution is adopted. Two aspects of state organisation on which public feelings run very high are: education and the health service. This underlines the need for effective criteria to judge efficiency of state organisations. Table 9.6 identifies some criteria that may be used for judging the efficiency of state organisations. The weakness of the criteria postulated is that the same criteria cannot be applied to every case. To try to overcome this problem two-factor criteria have been proposed which relate cost to some vital characteristics of the activity. This gives one way

TABLE 9.6 Possible criteria for judging the efficiency of state organisations

Type of organisation	Possible criteria for judging efficiency
Advising on policy developments	The cost of advisers could be compared with the cost of consultants operating in the open market preparing similar studies. The daily cost of a professional in a state organisation could be compared with the daily cost of consultants operating in the open market. Advising a major international company on its future policy is very similar to advising a government on policy.
Organisation with factory-like output (this could include activities like education and health services)	The cost per unit produced – this can be compared with the cost per unit of other producers of similar outputs. For example if the state produces electricity the cost could be compared with that of other producers in terms of cost per kilowatt-hour of electricity produced.
An organisation that has some national security role	The problem of finding a way of comparing the cost of providing any form of national security service is difficult, as there is no direct comparison with activities in the commercial world. One possible solution is to compare expenditure per head of population with that of other countries with a similar standard of living and a similar political outlook. This does not really prove efficiency or give any measure of the effectiveness of the expenditure.
An organisation that is responsible for gathering intelligence of a confidential nature	This is also a case where there is no direct comparison with the commercial world. So like the case above of an organisation that has some national security role the most useful way of comparing efficiency is by comparison with countries of a similar standard of living and similar political outlook. The importance of a similar political outlook must be stressed as the expenditure in a dictatorship running a police state would be quite different to an open democratic society.

TABLE 9.7 Summary of the benefits of testing the acceptability of the way a new activity is arranged

Aspect tested	Benefit
Equipment performance.	The adequacy of the specification of equipment proved.
Acceptability to the public.	The reaction of the public to the real activity as opposed to a paper proposal can be determined. Both objections and agreement can be better defined.
Costs can be assessed more accurately.	A trial should give a more accurate estimate of the real cost of fully implementing the proposal.
Real benefits can be determined more accurately.	The real benefits, if any, of the activity can be more accurately determined from a trial than from a paper exercise.
Proposed management and operational structure can be assessed.	Any weaknesses in the proposed management and operational structure can be identified and remedied.

of comparing possible alternative lines of expenditure, but it does not give any measure of customer satisfaction or quality of output.

It is recognised that the assessment of the acceptability of the efficiency of an activity may take place both when an activity is proposed and when it is in operation.

Assessment of the acceptability of an activity at the proposal stage allows the full range of factors involved to be considered and the design of the activity to be adjusted for maximum efficiency. Unfortunately at the design stage the quality of information on which decisions have to be based may not be very high. This problem may be overcome by running some kind of trial of the activity. A trial may be difficult to arrange particularly if legislation specifies an activity has to start on a particular date, or the activity is new. Difficulties should not be used as an excuse for not having a trial. There are usually many benefits from holding a trial. The potential benefits of a trial are summarised in Table 9.7.

General comments

The discussion so far has concentrated on: (1) showing the differences between private and state organisations in the scope there is for measuring efficiency; and (2) identifying methods that may be used to measure efficiency in both types of organisation. In this section a discussion is given of the efficacy of the various methods of measuring efficiency.

At the heart of any method of measuring the efficiency of an activity is measurement of the return on the capital or capital equivalent at risk (Bessis 1999). It is recognised that the method may not state the measurement directly in terms of return on capital. In commercial operations it may be relatively easy to identify the return on capital at risk. With state operations it is, as already hinted, difficult to find a measure of return on capital when provision of non-price goods or services is involved. The exercise becomes more difficult when a way of expressing the return on capital at risk has to be found for comparing efficiency of spending on different types of non-price goods. The most important condition is that such comparisons are made on a consistent basis.

Another situation that is difficult to deal with is when the return on expenditure on novel projects has to be compared with more conventional forms of expenditure. It could be that an allowance for the novelty of the project is factored into the comparison. The novelty factor must be clearly stated, in a way that is easily understood by all concerned. Such an approach is easier to state than to implement. Not all novelty is the same, it could be considered that there are degrees of novelty. Some novel activities, such as building a new aeroplane, might involve several major programmes of basic research taking several years and being run in parallel with the main programme. The results of such research may show the whole project has to be redesigned. Overall efficiency may be improved by a redesign of the project.

Assessment of efficiency, like many other things in life, is subject to change. An assessment is only right for the time at which it is made. If an assessment is made today, it is likely to be out of date next month and even more out of date next year. With time every variable is likely to change. Changes in variables are just one of the manifestations of risk that entrepreneurs have to accept as part of their way of life.

Earlier it was shown how many technical developments have changed most people's way of life with the direct consequences on patterns of demand. The case with which changes can be made to satisfy new demands can be subject to assessment of the efficiency with which the change can be made. Efficiency could be measured in terms of cost of time. It might be more effective to take account of both cost and time.

In Table 9.8 the various factors that have to be considered in assessing the efficiency of any activity are summarised and an indication is given of the efficacy of the associated assessment.

TABLE 9.8 Summary of the efficacy of various factors used in the assessment of the efficiency of an activity

Assessment factor	Efficacy
Cost	If limited to just cost in direct money terms, does not take into account non-monetary variables like market share, future markets and flexibility.
Benefits	Difficult to quantify total benefits – some benefits may be non-price benefits.
Net-benefit	Better than just cost or benefit.
Through life net benefit	Gives a through life assessment but may be difficult to evaluate the significance of all the changes that take place through life.
Flexibility	This only shows how adaptable to change a particular activity is, it does not measure return earned.
Through life return on capital used	This has many advantages provided the analysis takes account of through life changes in demand and market share. The method does not give an indication of the magnitude of uncertainties associated with changes in demand, but this can be tailored into the analysis.

Conclusions

The main functions of management are: target setting, problem solving, leadership, team building and understanding the implication of the risks involved.

Essentially the efficiency of any management system whether in private industry or state service is measured by the way it ensures targets are satisfied, the speed with which problems are solved and that appropriate arrangements are made for future developments. In private industry efficiency tends ultimately to be judged on the basis of the return on capital put at risk.

One very important benefit of measuring performance/efficiency is that it exposes where improvement in efficiency can be made.

There are no universal criteria for measuring efficiency. Appropriate criteria generally contain two factors, money and an activity characteristic. The money factor does give one basis for comparing options within a particular type of activity. Because the aims and purposes of some activities are very different it is not really possible to compare their total value to the community except in money terms.

Performance of activities in the commercial sector can generally be judged in terms of increased market share, increased turnover and increased profit. The same criteria are not practical for state organisations. Some state activities such as those that have a factory-like output may benefit from privatisation. The efficiency of state organisations can often only be assessed by comparison with other similar organisations. In the case of novel activities the inherent problems and the potential efficiency can often be identified by a small-scale trial of the activity before a commitment is made to putting the activity into full operation.

The potential efficiency of an activity should be assessed at the conceptual stage and should be kept under review throughout the activity's life. Some actions that can be taken to improve the performance of managers are:

1   Improve the quality of managers employed.

2   Establish criteria for measuring performance and regularly measure performance against the criteria.

3   The criteria for measuring performance must be tailored to suit the particular activity involved. In some cases cost can be used as the basis for measuring performance. In the case of non-traded goods measuring performance becomes more subjective and ideally should be based on a judgement of through life benefit. Whatever criteria are adopted they must be used consistently and checked if possible by comparing them against similar indicators in other countries.

4   Improve quality of output and reduce the cost of achieving quality.

5   In state activities assess whether privatisation is likely to improve overall efficiency.

6   The potential efficiency of an activity should be assessed when it is proposed and monitored when it is operating.

7   The potential efficiency of a major activity can often be realistically assessed by a trial of the proposed activity. Such a trial may often show how efficiency can be improved in the full operation of the activity.

The measurement of the efficiency of an organisation, whether a private industry organisation or state activity, will provide a consistent way of assessing the extent to which the organisation satisfies the essential requirements of sound entrepreneurism.

When there is some measure of efficiency it will give an indication of the value of changes that have to be made to improve efficiency and an indication of the value of alternatives.

The contribution that entrepreneurism will make is in determining which risk options are most acceptable.

Reference

Bessis, J. (1995) *Risk Management in Banking*, Chichester: John Wiley and Sons, reprinted 1999, pp. 262–75.

CHAPTER TEN

Conclusions

The aim of this book was set as identifying the contribution of entrepreneurial philosophy to good management in both the public and private sectors. It was recognised from the beginning that there are considerable differences between the operating environments of the two sectors. At the same time it was recognised that despite the differences there are management functions that are common to both sectors. It was also recognised that because of the many common interfaces between the two sectors managers in each sector have to have an understanding of how the other sector works and the constraints on the way they operate.

The important characteristics of both private and public organisations are summarised in Table 10.1. The essential tools of management are summarised in Table 10.2. In Table 10.2 the term Work Study is included. It is appreciated that the term has been around for a long time, but it is considered a very important tool of all management that is often not given sufficient recognition. An important implication of the term work study is that it requires the manager to understand the whole process of the activity he/she is managing. It is only when a process is thoroughly understood that the scope for improvements can be identified. It is a primary responsibility of any manager to seek out and implement improvements in efficiency; failure to implement improvements in efficiency is likely to lead to an organisation being replaced by a more efficient one.

Examples of the action needed to improve efficiency are elimination of the creeping paralysis of the proliferation of committees in the public sector and the revitalisation of geriatric companies in the private sector. No organisation can ever allow a committee to be formed or continue to exist unless its efficiency is tested and found to be acceptable. Equally no company that does not have active and dynamic plans for its future development can continue to exist.

TABLE 10.1 The essential characteristics of public and private organisations

Type of organisation	Essential characteristics
Central government	Function:
	Implementing legislation and advising government
	Constraints:
	Has to be sensitive to the political climate Has to operate within a fixed budget
Local government	Function:
	Has to satisfy central government policy and satisfy the needs of the local community
	Constraints:
	Has to work within budget limits set by central government Has to be sensitive to local demands Has to work closely with local elected members
Private sector	Function:
	To provide goods and services demanded by the public in a way that will show a profit and help the company grow
	Constraints:
	The resources of the company The capability of the workforce The ability of the company to finance its activities either from its own resources or by borrowing The constraints placed on its operations by government

Ensuring the efficiency of operations is the function of management that is vital to both public and private sector organisations. It is also the feature of the entrepreneurial approach which is particularly important, as the process of measuring performance often exposes just where improvements in efficiency can be made.

The main conclusions drawn in this study are:

1   The entrepreneurial role of managers is different in the civil service, local government and private industry. But there are important advantages in managers in one environment understanding the way managers in other environments work, as there are likely to be circumstances where they interface.

TABLE 10.2 The essential tools for all managers

Tools	Purpose
Leadership (open minded with a critical outlook)	To encourage teams to work in the most effective way and to ensure they know what has to be done.
Target setting	To identify what has to be done by when and within what cost constraints.
Communication	To be able to communicate with all concerned with the activity in the most effective way and with the least chance of misunderstanding.
Problem solving (including dealing with crises)	This is in many ways the most important tool of managers. An effective manager must be able to deal with all the problems that may arise in a particular activity.
Obtaining resources	A manager must be able to obtain resources of the quality required to ensure an activity is completed in the way required and to the time specified.
Progressing work	A manager must be able to monitor progress of an activity in detail, so that any problems can be dealt with as soon as possible, thus reducing their potential for harming the activity.
Work study/operational research	Assessing what has to be done so that the most efficient way of completing the task can be identified.
Thinking ahead	What will be required in future years? What changes will have to be made to deal with future conditions?
Risk assessment	Identifying the range of risks involved and determining their acceptability.

2   For all managers there is a common core of interests. These interests
     include understanding:

- the product

- demand

- the constraints on supply of the product

- the problems with obtaining resources to produce the product
  in the volume required to satisfy demand

- requirements for staff and their training

- the regulations that have to be satisfied

- the adequacy of finance for future developments

- the impact of competition

- dealing with crises

The review of various aspects of management has underlined certain characteristics that are essential to good management in both the public and private sectors. In both sectors there is an important but different element of entrepreneurism, the element being more direct and central to the private sector. However, entrepreneurism is also very important to the public sector. The enormous sums of money spent in the public sector on supplies exposes the scope for entrepreneurism in the public sector. Characteristics considered essential to all good management procedures include:

1   An in-depth understanding of the product being dealt with.

2   An ability to lead the team involved and ensure that they are developed to perform in the most efficient way possible.

3   An ability to solve the problems that may occur.

4   To be able to organise an appropriate response to crisis situations, ranging from fires to bomb threats and from loss of markets to failure of products.

5   To be able to plan the future development of an organisation.

In-depth understanding of the product means that the manager must understand the product and the implications of every facet of the product, whatever form the product takes, whether it is building a car, producing a new food product or in the public sector managing a form of tax collection or building a new road.

One very important skill common to management in both the private and public sectors is understanding the philosophy of risk assessment and risk management. Understanding the philosophy of risk assessment is part of the foundation of management entrepreneurism. Assessment of risk is not just confined to technical issues, but applies equally to organisational issues. An important function of management is to assess the magnitude and acceptability of the risks associated with every activity they are responsible for. Table 10.3 illustrates the range of risk management has to assess.

Evaluation of risk acceptability is at the heart of all decision making. Determining what risk is acceptable is the essential function of an

TABLE 10.3 Examples of the range of risk management has to assess and manage

Risks	Some of the factors involved
Technical	Will product satisfy performance, reliability and quality specification requirements?
Market	How large and how stable is the market? What changes may take place in the market?
Supply	What are the consequences of failure of supplies? Are alternative suppliers available and at what cost?
Asset	What is the potential impact of the proposed activity on the organisation's assets?
Credit	What is the impact of lenders or borrowers becoming insolvent?
Interest rate	What would be the impact of upward and downward changes in interest rates?
Foreign exchange	What would be the impact of upward and downward changes in exchange rates?
Funding	What chance is there that funding plans will fail?
Security	Are the risks of fraud or robbery known and acceptable or is action required to reduce them?

entrepreneur. Some entrepreneurs may be risk takers and some may be risk averse. An entrepreneur's approach to risk taking to a very large extent defines their style of management.

Table 10.3 is not intended to be a comprehensive list of all the risks that have to be considered in an activity or project but merely to indicate the range of risk factors that should be considered. Each factor mentioned consists of many sub-factors which each have to be considered. Table 10.4 shows the sub-factors that are likely to be considered in the assessment of a technical factor.

The merit of risk assessment and risk management as tools for the entrepreneurial manager is that they make the manager aware of the uncertainties he/she must allow for.

It is not suggested that risk assessment gives exact answers, the answers it gives are only as good as the evidence they are based on. An important benefit of risk assessment is that it exposes weaknesses in the data used and the implications of such weaknesses. For example the statistical distribution of data that has to be used may be unknown. Some of the possible forms of data distribution are shown in Figure 10.1.

TABLE 10.4 Technical sub-factors' risk likely to require assessment

Sub-factor	Aspect needing assessment
Performance does not satisfy specification.	Action needed to make project successful.
Cost of providing sub-factor too high.	How can costs be reduced.
Producing sub-factor not possible with resources available.	Alternative sub-factor to be found.
Materials supplied contain too many defects.	Supplier of material of the required quality to be found.
Manufacture involves use of toxic materials which are difficult to contain.	Alternative non-toxic material to be found.
Problem in getting Health and Safety Executive approval for novel project.	Additional effort to be devoted to getting approval from Health and Safety Executive.
Expensive to dispose of waste products produced.	Way of disposing safely of waste products produced.
Problems with development of product make funds uncertain for financing project further.	Other sources of finance to be found.

FIGURE 10.1 Some possible forms of data distribution

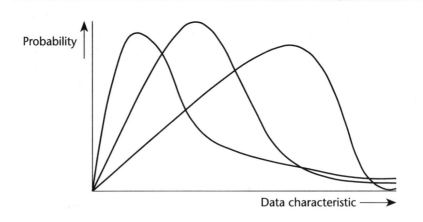

FIGURE 10.2   The possible impact of improved data on assessment

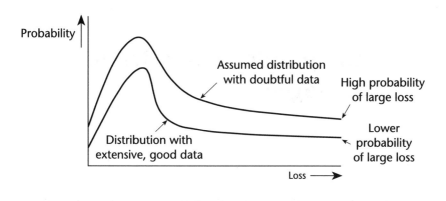

The data of interest may be measures of any of a huge range of characteristics. The range includes: loss of profit, loss of market, failure of performance, loss of production, failure of funding and loss of key workers.

In modelling any potential risk situation the implications of possible variation of distribution must be allowed for. As real data precisely related to the particular situation of interest becomes available understanding of the significance of uncertainty becomes more precise. This situation is illustrated diagrammatically in Figure 10.2.

It has to be appreciated that improved data may show that the probability of a large loss can be either higher or lower than the prediction based on doubtful data. It also has to be recognised that the probability of a high loss may be an inherent characteristic of some activities.

The problems of selecting managers

The first step in selecting a manager is to decide what you want the manager to do. Not all managers have to have the same range of skills, capability and experience. The manager of the post room in a government office requires a somewhat simpler range of skills than the manager of a car factory or the manager of a chemical plant design office.

Whatever the form of recruitment and whether it is internal or external, there are five steps in the recruitment process:

1   Define duties to be performed.

2   Ask interested parties a number of questions that define the adequacy of their education, training, experience and a general fitness for the job. Some of the questions may be asked in the initial advertisement of the vacancy or in a standardised application form that all applicants are asked to complete.

3   Assess applications to determine which candidates appear worth interviewing. A simple form setting out the range of information required and recording assessment of the information obtained from the various applicants is shown in Figure A1.1. The acceptability of the answers should be rated in a consistent way and the rating recorded on the form.

4   Interview the candidates that seem to satisfy the requirements. A from that may be adapted for comparing the assessments of the acceptability of the candidates is shown in Figure A1.2. The score allocated takes into account the information given in the application form and any interview or tests.

5   Offer the job to the candidate that is considered most acceptable.

FIGURE A1.1 Simple form setting out questions to be answered about a candidate

No	Criteria	Method of checking*		
		App. form	Interview	Test
	Skills and abilities			
1.	Ability to work on own initiative with minimum supervision and guidance to agreed time-scales and targets.			
2.	Ability to identify needs of the department and balance them with organisational constraints.			
3.	Ability to formulate and present policies with clear and justified recommendations.			
4.	Ability to review existing practices and provide recommendations and alternatives.			
5.	Ability to influence, guide and advise other managers.			
6.	Ability to make effective contact with staff and directors.			
	Experience			
7.	Minimum of two years' experience in similar post.			
	Knowledge			
8.	Thorough knowledge and understanding of processes involved including use of computers.			
	Education, training and qualifications			
9.	Degree.			
10.	Professional qualification.			
	Management competencies/special requirements			
11.	Sets and meets challenging objectives.			
12.	Takes responsibility of ensuring plans and ideas are delivered.			
13.	Makes decisions in a confidential and understanding way, even when faced with difficult situations or threats.			
	Personal impact			
14.	Structures and conveys ideas and information which result in clarity/understanding and impact.			

*The acceptability of candidates' response is rated on a scale of 1 to 4. The definition of the points on the scale are:

1 Acceptable without question
2 Acceptable with minor reservations
3 Major reservations
4 Completely unacceptable

FIGURE A1.2 Form for comparing final assessments of candidates

Assesment criteria	Names of applicants									
	1	2	3	4	5	6	7	8	9	10
	Please insert the appropriate score code: 1 Acceptable without question 2 Acceptable with some reservations 3 Major reservations 4 Completely unacceptable									
Skills and abilities										
Experience										
Knowledge										
Education, training and qualification										
Management competence										
Personal impact										
Total score										

Generally the initial performance of a new manager has to be monitored fairly carefully to ensure that he/she is really capable of doing the job.

For some jobs the candidate may be tested in detail. For example capability to operate a computer might be tested, a teacher or lecturer might be asked to give a trial lecture before a team of assessors, a medical doctor's competence might be evaluated by assessing the success of his/her treatments, a pilot's capability might be checked by testing his/her performance in a flight simulator. For someone who would have to undergo a long and expensive training before they become operationally effective the assessment might be longer and involve some form of psychometric testing. Such testing can be particularly useful in determining if someone is able to deal with a particularly stressful job.

Additional tests that should be made as a matter of good practice are: medical check on the applicant's health and a check that the person has not got a criminal record.

The nature of quality assurance controls

In this appendix the management implications of quality assurance procedures are examined. It is stressed the points made apply to organisations in both the public and private sector. To prevent any misunderstanding quality assurance is defined as Odgers of British Telecom has defined total quality management: as a 'policy of meeting customer's requirements first time every time at the lowest cost' (Odgers 1990). Such a policy requires that:

> It must apply to all functions within an organisation and be directed in a way which seeks to maximise customer satisfaction for the 'product' of that function. How performance or satisfaction is measured obviously depends on the function being considered and quantifiable measures may be difficult to establish when dealing with the public sector activities like welfare payments or defence expenditure. Failure to deal effectively with quality problems may lead to: loss of customers, or loss of jobs or, as was reported for Mazda, salary cuts for senior executives. (Helm 1990: 11).

In the following the examination of quality assurance management procedures is divided into four parts: the basic role of management, the requirement of quality assurance management controls, obstacles to effective use of quality assurance management and results of introducing effective quality assurance management.

The basic role of management

The basic role of management in any organisation is to ensure that the objectives of the organisation are satisfied as efficiently as possible. The management function set is part of the greater social society set and as such the management functions have to respond to changes in the social society set. The set of functions that management has to perform in order to satisfy this role can generally be summarised under six headings, which are shown diagrammatically in Figure A2.1. In practice the six functions are not mutually exclusive and there is generally a certain amount of overlap. The amount of overlap depends on the way managers' responsibilities are allocated and the way managers discharge their duties.

The six management functions identified need to be described in rather more detail so that their role in the overall management system can be appreciated.

Responsibility for profitable operation means it is management's responsibility to ensure that the product/service that is produced is one

FIGURE A2.1   Diagrammatic representation of management functions

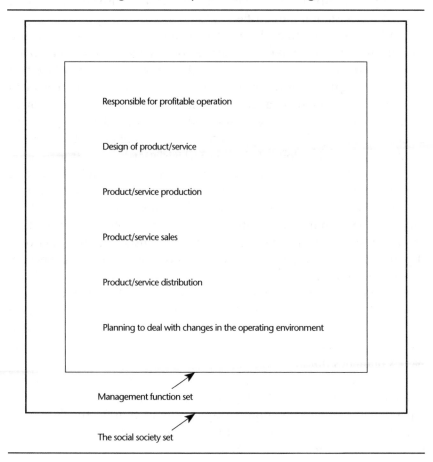

Responsible for profitable operation

Design of product/service

Product/service production

Product/service sales

Product/service distribution

Planning to deal with changes in the operating environment

Management function set

The social society set

for which there is a demand and one which can be produced at a price that will yield an acceptable level of profit. In the public sector profitable operation as a measure of successful operation may be replaced simply by client satisfaction at minimum cost.

Design of product/service means the comprehensive responsibility for ensuring the product/service involved satisfies the market and all the regulatory requirements associated with such products. It has to be recognised that in the public sector the market may be defined by legislation.

Product/service production simply means production of the product/service concerned in the quality and numbers required by the market. Both under- and over-production in the private sector can mean less than optimum profit from the operation and in the public sector less satisfaction of clients.

The product/service sales function in the private sector simply means organising capture of the optimum share of the market to match a company's capacity. In the public sector this means ensuring that clients defined by legislation are satisfied.

When planning to deal with change in the operating environment, the private sector concern is concentrated on changes that may take place in the market. It has to be remembered that these changes may be either positive or negative. Positive changes are those that lead to an increase in demand, while negative changes are those that either cause a reduction in demand or introduce massive claims for damage suffered due to problems associated with products supplied earlier. The public sector concern would be the implications of changes in legislation.

In any description of the organisation of a company it is easy to give the impression that just establishing the appropriately named departments will ensure that everyone involved will instinctively co-operate to produce a harmonious organisation devoted to promoting the interests of the organisation. In practice there can be intensive struggles between departments defending their assumed territory. Such struggles generally damage the efficiency of a company.

Salutory examples of the quality assurance problems management may be faced with are: the $7 million fine Ford paid for falsifying emission test records (Helm 1990: 11) and the president of the Sumitomo Bank stepping down because of illegal activities by the head of one of the Bank's branches (ibid.).

It is a basic tenet of the arguments that follow that quality assurance is an integral function of all phases of management and not some separate independent function. To lay the foundation for the discussion that follows Table A2.1 identifies the main quality assurance controls of each of the main management functions.

TABLE A2.1 Quality assurance control elements of management functions

Management function responsibility	Quality assurance controls
Profitable operation	Ensuring the product satisfies the customer at a profitable price
Design of product	Ensuring design of product satisfies market and regulatory requirements
Product production	Ensuring product consistently satisfies customer and regulatory requirements
Product sales	Ensuring the product is distributed in the most efficient way
Changes in operating environment	Ensuring that optimum benefit is derived from changes in the operating environment

The requirements of quality assurance management controls

Examination of the requirements for total quality management control is in many ways nothing more than good business management. Good business management requires that a company directs all its efforts to maximising profits, staying in business and expanding business where possible. Something of the difference between a company without quality assurance controls and a company with complete quality assurance controls is shown in Table A2.2. The change from an organisation without a quality assurance approach to one with a total quality assurance approach can only be achieved if the senior management is totally committed and everyone concerned is appropriately educated and trained. The chief executive must take responsibility for and believe in total quality assurance management. It is his/her responsibility to ensure that departmental barriers are brought down and that everyone has a clear understanding of the needs of their customers. Acceptability of everyone's performance will be measured by the extent to which customers' needs are satisfied. Involving everyone in quality management will improve the overall effectiveness of the company. Executives must devote time to ensuring that the precepts of total quality assurance are being followed. Total quality assurance management philosophy is not intended as a 'quick fix' but a long-term commitment to improvement and adaptation to a changing world.

TABLE A2.2 Differences between companies with and without quality assurance controls

Management function responsibility	Company without quality assurance management controls	Company with quality assurance management controls
Profitable organisation	Profit at risk due to quality	Customer satisfaction brings profits
Design of product	Design uncoordinated, requires extensive development	All departments involved in design, which results in reduced development time
Product production	Proportion of defects/ faults high	Defect/fault rate low
Product sales	High rate of complaints	Customers' satisfaction is high
Product distribution	Customers' delivery requirements not considered	Product available when required
Changes in operating environment	Inflexible approach to change	Adapts to changing circumstances

Maximum benefits only result from an organisation working as a team in a controlled and planned way. Like any team everyone has to be trained to understand their role and the contribution they are expected to make. As with any successful team, members of the team must be fully committed to the team. Some of the benefits of team commitment are:

- Each team member focused on 'his' customers

- Everyone belongs to the team aimed at satisfying the customer

- Individual responsibility for satisfying customers

- Constant challenge to improve product or service to customer

- Teamwork produces a unified approach to satisfying customers

How the effectiveness of the management function can be assessed is not discussed in detail in this appendix. But often some form of ranking is appropriate. The problems associated with ranking are described in Chicken (1996).

Obstacles to effective use of quality assurance management principles

Six main types of obstacle to the effective use of a total quality approach can be identified, and they are summarised in Table A2.3. Policy not being properly understood is often a cause of the ineffective implementation of an otherwise sound quality assurance policy. Poor communication between the various parties involved is often the reason for the policy not being followed.

In some organisations that have been operating in a very routine way for several years the whole organisation tends to adopt an inflexible attitude towards change. This fear of change needs radical treatment to involve the whole team and make them appreciate the need for change.

Many cases of grandiose schemes for quality assurance management, which are introduced with a great flourish and the distribution of a multi-volume description of the scheme, fail. The descriptions of the scheme tend to stay unread. This results in the scheme never being made fully operational.

Lack of interest in quality assurance controls could be considered as a variation of the inflexible team syndrome mentioned earlier. But it also contains the element of apathy towards the introduction of any new procedure or process. To overcome such apathy generally requires drastic action at the most senior level.

TABLE A2.3   Main types of obstacle to implementation of a total quality approach

Type of obstacle	Characteristic cause
Quality assurance policy not understood	Lack of adequate training
Established practices prevent adoption of policy	Benefits of quality assurance policy not appreciated
Policy specified in a complicated way	Team not involved in developing policy
Lack of interest in quality assurance	Senior management not committed
Team not trained in appropriate methods	Organisation's inadequate commitment to training
Policy falls into disuse	Chief executive not committed

Lack of training is an obstacle that should never arise in a well-managed organisation. It is a fundamental feature of good management that everyone in an organisation is trained in the duties they have to perform. Such training starts with the cleaners and includes every grade in the organisation. We all know what a bad impression on customers can be created by a badly trained receptionist, who does not even know the main people in the organisation. Training is not a once-only operation but something that continues throughout a person's working life and is an essential way of introducing new policies and procedures. The training does not necessarily have to be of the classroom type, it could be a workshop-type presentation with a facilitator-led discussion (Harvey Jones 1988: 282).

Quality assurance control policy failing by falling into disuse is most likely to be due to either a lack of commitment or the policy not being practical. Such failure must be the responsibility of the chief executive who should have detected the problem when the scheme was being introduced.

The results of introducing effective quality assurance management control

Sound quality assurance controls will transform an organisation. Functional barriers will disappear and management will ensure departments interact effectively. Quality improvements will be seen as a vital part of each employee's job and management will provide the tools, training support and direction to the quality environment of the organisation.

References

Chicken, J.C. (1996) *Risk Handbook*, London: International Thomson Business Press.

Harvey Jones, J. (1988) *Making it Happen*, London: Fontana, p. 282.

Helm, L. (1990) 'Mazda makes an act of contribution for car flaws', *International Herald Tribune* 29–30 December, p. 11.

Odgers, G.D.W. (1990) 'Total Quality and "high wire" performance', *Institution of Mechanical Engineers*, second Hugh Ford Management Lecture, November 1989, I.Mech.E., Preprint No. 4.

Selvidge, J.E. (1990) 'Corporate management of liability risk', published in Louis A. Cox and Paolo F. Ricci (eds), *New Risks Issues and Management*, New York: Plenum Press, p. 12.

Assessment of the acceptability of projects

The problem of assessing and making decisions about the acceptability of projects is discussed at some length in Chicken (1994, 1996), and more recently in a study called *RAMP* (*Risk Analysis and Management for Projects*) made by the Institution of Civil Engineers, the Institute of Actuaries and the Faculty of Actuaries (1999). Many discussions about decision making relate the acceptability of a course of action to the option that offers the greatest return in money terms at an acceptable level of risk. There are also many types of project, particularly those involving government expenditure, where the return cannot be measured accurately in money terms (Chicken 1994). In the following it is assumed that it is possible to describe the risks associated with a project in terms of money and probability.

Setting the level of risk that is acceptable is at the heart of determining what is acceptable. It is also at the centre of defining the range of management responsibilities. Put in another way, whatever problems arise it is management's responsibility to find solutions that keep risks to an acceptable level taking account of all the technical economic and socio-political factors involved.

It is possible to structure the analysis of the options open as shown in Figure A3.1. The risk causes considered must include the socio-political factors. Consistent criteria for assessing the range of socio-political factors involved must be derived. General guidance on consistent assessment of socio-political factors is given in Chicken (1994).

For any particular activity the methodology for calculating the leverages of the costs of making the risks involved acceptable is demonstrated in Figure A3.2. The cost of making a risk acceptable is defined as the total cost, that is the sum of all the expenditure necessary to deal with the risk involved in a way that will allow the specification set for the proposal/project to be satisfied.

FIGURE A3.1 Structure of analysis of risks associated with an activity

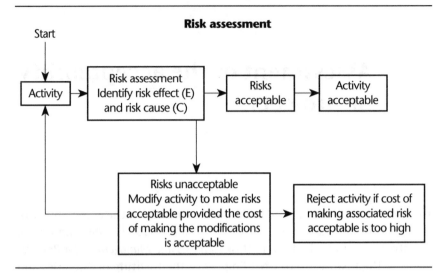

References

Chicken, J.C. (1994) *Managing Risk and Decisions in Major Projects*, London: Chapman and Hall.

Chicken J.C. (1996) *Risk Handbook*, London: International Thomson Business Press.

Ramp (Risk Analysis and Management for Projects) (1999) a report prepared by the Institution of Civil Engineers, Faculty of Actuaries and the Institute of Actuaries, London: Thomas Telford Publishing.

Koutsoyiannis, A. (1982) *Non-price Decisions: The Firm in a Modern Context*, London: Macmillan.

FIGURE A3.2 Evaluation of risk leverage

Risk	Cost (x)	Probability (p)	px
Risk 1	x_1	p_1	$p_1 x_1$
Risk 2	x_2	p_2	$p_2 x_2$
Risk n	x_n	p_n	$p_n x_n$

conventional decision theory makes judgement on these values

TOTAL COST $\sum_n^1 x$ TOTAL RISK $\sum_n^1 px$

$$L = \text{risk leverage} = \frac{\dfrac{\sum_n^1 px}{n} - px \text{ (of interest)}}{px \text{ (of interest)}}$$

For a particular project the acceptability of various levels of leverage has to be agreed

Decision levels for L

If L is more than 2 risk is generally acceptable
If L is between 0 and below 2 judgement needed to decide if action is required
If L is negative the risk is unacceptable and action would be required to reduce the risk to a more acceptable level

In cases where L is between 0 and below 2 it is possible to develop specific guidance on how the judgement about acceptability can be made. The guidance would to some extent depend on the perception of the level of acceptable risk. In general terms the risk leverage level L defines the priority that should be given to dealing with the various risks involved

Social cost-benefit analysis

Assessment of the acceptability of proposals for which there is not a quantifiable output makes analysis in cost-benefit terms difficult. Such cases often arise when the output is described in social terms. One approach to solving this problem is to use some form of social cost-benefit analysis (SCBA).

One basis for comparison of investment options is to calculate the net benefit (NB) on the basis of the resulting exports X, imports M and domestic inputs D.

$$\text{Then NB} = X - M - D \text{ where } X, M \text{ and } D \text{ are valued in consistent currency.}$$

For a proposal to be acceptable, NB would have to be greater than 0. If several options have to be considered, the option that would be most acceptable would be the one that showed the greatest NB. The problems associated with assessing the acceptability of the social benefit of investment proposals in other countries are:

■ doubts about the stability of the exchange rate;

■ reliable assessment of the impact of protective practices such as tariffs, quota restrictions and subsidies;

■ availability of labour with appropriate skills;

■ availability of all the required support services.

The list of associated problems shows how using X, M and D, in the simple way described above, exposes the potential sources of error in the calculation which, as far as possible, have to be eliminated in as effective and consistent a way as possible. One way, but not a perfect way, of dealing with the problem is to use weighting factors to emphasise the relative significance of each problem factor. Such weighting factors may introduce other problems, particularly if they are derived subjectively.

Assuming that the weighting factors can be used with confidence, the net benefit equation could be written as follows:

$$NB = a(bcdX - bM - cdD)$$

Where a is the weighting factor for exchange rate stability

b is the weighting factor for impact of protective practices

c is the weighting factor for labour availability

d is the weighting factor for adequacy of support services

X, M and D are as defined earlier

Economic cost-benefit analysis

The above equation gives a hint of the significance of the efficiency of pricing which has to be considered in economic cost-benefit analysis (ECBA). But that is not the only feature that has to be considered in assessing the economic acceptability of projects in the public sector. It is sometimes convenient to consider projects from three aspects:

1   financial profitability, measured in market prices;

2   economic profitability, measured in efficiency prices;

3   social profitability, measured in social prices.

Evaluation of projects based on non-traded goods

To evaluate a project for which the output cannot be measured directly in market price terms, because the output is in the form of some non-traded good, is surrounded by difficulties. In such cases the composition of the costs involved should, as far as possible, be broken down into its component parts such as traded goods, services and labour. Even when the components are identified, there may be problems in pricing them, as some may have no traded price analogue. A method of converting market prices into economic or social prices is sometimes accomplished using 'accounting ratios' (ARs). Various conventions have been proposed for making such conversions: some just consider single goods, others adopt average conversion factors for a group of factors. These variations in conventions together with the variations in exchange rates, prices and taxes all underline the magnitude of uncertainties that have to be allowed for in making an assessment of the acceptability of a project.

Social opportunity cost

Public expenditure can sometimes be evaluated in terms of social opportunity cost. In assessing the implications of social pricing, consideration has to be given to the weighting that should be adopted to allow for distribution of benefits. An egalitarian view that all benefits are equal, no matter where they arise, is not entirely satisfactory. Weighting of the importance of a project also has to consider the time and place the benefits will arise – it is possible more value may be attributed to benefits that arise in the immediate future than those that will arise a long time into the future.

Weighting of factors

The specification of weights has in some way to reflect what is the desired distribution of benefits. The desired distribution may be quite different to the present distribution and it may be skewed in favour of a particular section of the population. Whatever the distribution that is decided upon, it must be defensible both in terms of the evidence on which it is based and its appropriateness to the people who will be exposed to the project. For example, it may be expected that consumption is to have an optimum value N. Following the rules of diminishing marginal utility of extra consumption, if only lower consumption is possible, it would have marginally higher value N_1 and if only higher consumption was possible it would have a marginally lower value N_2. For such a pattern of benefits, a justifiable system of weighting could be for consumption level N weighting to be 1, for consumption level N_1 weighting to be greater than 1 and for consumption level N_2 weighting to be less than 1. Exactly how much the weighting of N_1 and N_2 would be above and below 1 would depend on the details of each specific case.

If a project is aimed at producing major structural changes in the pattern of a particular county's economy, or a company's structure, then it would be appropriate to weight the various options according to the likelihood that they would produce the required changes. It can be appreciated that proposals that make a positive contribution to achieving the required structural change should be given a weighting that would increase their acceptability. Proposals that would make a negative contribution to achieving the required structural change should be given a weighting that would reduce their acceptability. Quantifying such weightings would involve a considerable amount of judgement, which would have a large subjective component and involve a considerable amount of policy making.

Index